A PRACTICAL GUIDE TO

EARLY CHILDHOOD STUDIES GRADUATE PRACTITIONER COMPETENCIES

Sara Miller McCune founded Sage Publishing in 1965 to support the dissemination of usable knowledge and educate a global community. Sage publishes more than 1,000 journals and over 800 new books each year, spanning a wide range of subject areas. Our growing selection of library products includes archives, data, case studies and video. Sage remains majority owned by our founder and after her lifetime will become owned by a charitable trust that secures the company's continued independence.

Los Angeles | London | New Delhi | Singapore | Washington DC | Melbourne

A PRACTICAL GUIDE TO

EARLY CHILDHOOD STUDIES GRADUATE PRACTITIONER COMPETENCIES

EDITED BY
AARON BRADBURY
JACKIE MUSGRAVE
HELEN PERKINS

LM Learning Matters

Learning Matters
A Sage Publishing Company

Learning Matters
A Sage Publishing Company
1 Oliver's Yard
55 City Road
London EC1Y 1SP

Sage Publications Inc.
2455 Teller Road
Thousand Oaks, California 91320

Sage Publications India Pvt Ltd
B 1/I 1 Mohan Cooperative Industrial Area
Mathura Road
New Delhi 110 044

Sage Publications Asia-Pacific Pte Ltd
3 Church Street
#10-04 Samsung Hub
Singapore 049483

Library of Congress Control Number: 2023934019

British Library Cataloguing in Publication Data

A catalogue record for this book is available from the British Library

Editor: Amy Thornton
Senior project editor: Chris Marke
Project management: TNQ Technologies
Cover design: Wendy Scott
Typeset by: TNQ Technologies

ISBN: 978-1-5296-1872-3
ISBN: 978-1-5296-1871-6 (pbk)

CONTENTS

ABOUT THE EDITORS AND CONTRIBUTORS

ABOUT THE EDITORS

Aaron Bradbury is a Principal Lecturer for Early Years and Childhood (Learning and Development, Psychology, Special Educational Needs and Inclusion) at Nottingham Trent University. He is a Member of the Coalition for the Early Years on the Birth to 5 Matters and currently researching on early childhood workforce development. He has a passion for making the voice of the child, nurturing through a diverse lens and pioneers of early childhood the foreground of practice and he was a contributor to the development of the ECGPCs.

Jackie Musgrave Dr Jackie Musgrave is Associate Head of School with responsibility for Learning and Teaching in the School of Education, Childhood, Youth and Sport (ECYS) in the Faculty of Wellbeing, Education and Language Studies at the Open University. She leads on Academic Conduct in the School and co-chairs the Faculty wide Academic Integrity Implementation group. She is a Principal Fellow of Advance HE. Jackie completed her MA in Early Childhood Education and Doctor of Education at the University of Sheffield. Jackie's research explores issues relating to the health of babies and children, reflecting her previous professional experience as a general as well as paediatric nurse. Her research has explored how early years practitioners support the health of young children in early years settings. She is a member of the Executive for the Early Childhood Studies Degrees Network for the Research and Knowledge Exchange was a contributor to the development of the ECGPCs.

Helen Perkins is an Associate Lecturer at the Open University in Early Childhood Studies. She has been teaching early childhood education and care in further and higher education since 2002. She has experience working in the Early Years Foundation Stage and with children with additional needs. Helen has a Doctorate in Education (EdD, ECE); her research interest is centred on the professionalisation of the ECE workforce. Helen served as an expert panel member for the Nutbrown Review of Early Years qualifications. She is a member of the Executive for the Early Childhood Studies Degrees Network for the Research and Knowledge Exchange and an external examiner for Early Childhood Studies Degrees. Helen was a contributor to the development of the ECGPCs.

ABOUT THE AUTHORS

Tara Ball began her career in Early Years/primary education where she had experience of working across the entire Early Years/primary age range in both mixed and single age groups and teaching all subjects. She joined the Institute of Education at Staffordshire University in October 2014. She currently leads and teaches on the BA Hons Education, BA Hons Education (Early Years), BA Education (Post Compulsory in Education) top up and (also) on the master's in education as well as supervising undergraduate and post graduate research projects.

Heather Brammer worked in the NHS as a Nursery Nurse (on a Maternity Unit) and then later a Hospital Play Specialist for over 13 years. She has worked at two Further Education Colleges teaching, Childhood Studies, moving on to become a Course Team Leader for Child Studies awards. From 2006 she moved into Teacher Education working across a range of teaching programmes before finally, moving to Staffordshire University in 2015 to continue teaching on Early Childhood Studies.

Leanne Gray (EdD) is a Senior Lecturer in Education in the School of Education and Social Care at Anglia Ruskin University, United Kingdom. Her research interests focus on early childhood and mathematics education.

Selena Hall has taught Early Childhood studies for 16 years. Selena is a Lecturer on the BA (Hons) Early Childhood Studies and placement lead for the ECGPC. Selena is currently a member of the ECSDN Professionalism and Workforce strategy group. In relation to professional interests surrounding workforce development, Selena is currently supporting and advising other institutions who are introducing the ECGPC.

Dawn Jones is the course team leader for the BA (Hons) Early Childhood Studies programme with the embedded ECGPC and has been a lecturer in Early Years for 20 years. Dawn Jones research interests are situated within post-humanism and new materialism perspectives, in particular the intra-action of infants and the more-than-human world, also, sustainability within Early Years pedagogy and the voice and rights of young children.

David Meechan is a Lecturer at the University of Northampton. He has experience in private day nurseries and primary schools both in England and internationally. He has previously worked as a practitioner, class teacher and manager. David has two children currently under 6 and his wife is a Room Leader at a Nursery setting. He draws on his past and current experiences to promote a child rights-based approach to working with children and families.

Matt Northall has worked in higher education for the past 15 years, and prior to this, was employed in a variety of Early Years settings (private and state) before becoming a member of the senior leadership team at an inner-city school in the heart of the West Midlands.

Deborah Nye is a Lecturer at Coventry University and a researcher who works within the early childhood learning and development degree team. Her current doctorial research is in the indicative development of a child with dyslexia pre-diagnosis. Deborah has also taken part in the rewriting of the QAA standards as a reader and presented at several conferences nationally and internationally. Her undergraduate and master's degree are both in early childhood which is where her passion is rooted. Deborah is a member of the SEFDEY committee supporting the sector-endorsed foundation degree and supports as an external examiner on Early Years degrees.

Caroline Prior (Associate Professor Early Years Education) is a Senior Lecturer in the Education department at University College Birmingham (UCB). She is the Programme Lead for both the BA (Hons) Early Childhood Studies (Graduate Practitioner) and BA (Hons) Childhood and Education Studies (online) provision and is a strong advocate for early childhood with a passion and drive for securing better outcomes for both children and families.

Meredith Rose is a Course Leader for BA Early Childhood Studies and Senior Lecturer at NTU with 20 years of experience in leadership roles in Early Years practice, further and higher education. Meredith has research interests in graduate journeys, leadership and the recognition and value placed upon play-based pedagogy.

Stella Smith is a course leader for BA Early Years and has worked in the early childhood sector for the last 10 years. Stella began her career as an Early Years teacher in private day nurseries and then transitioning into further, then higher education. Stella has a passion for promoting positive attachments in Early Childhood Education and Care (ECEC).

Amanda Tayler began her career in Early Years as a parent helper in a small preschool. While there she gained her level 3 qualification and became a Nursery manager, then she studied for a foundation degree and level 6 top-up in Early Childhood Studies. While studying for her MA in Early Childhood Studies she became a course leader at a local college, then took a role at Staffordshire University where she is currently Course Leader for the full time BA (Hons) Early Childhood Studies. She is a Senior Fellow of the HEA and her doctoral research is looking at the role of the Early Years Teacher.

Philippa Thompson is a Principal Lecturer in Early Childhood Studies at Sheffield Hallam University and Co-Chair of the Early Childhood Studies Degree Network (ECSDN). Her research interests in early childhood include play, participation, co-production, outdoor learning and parents/children living with anaphylaxis. She has a strong practice background of 20 years across a broad range of settings in the United Kingdom and internationally. Philippa advocates regularly for changes to policy and practice and recognition for the sector and a graduate workforce.

Michelle Wisbey (EdD) is a Senior Lecturer in Early Years Education in the School of Education and Social Care at Anglia Ruskin University, United Kingdom. Her research interests focus on early childhood, Montessori approach to education and collaborative action right practice.

INTRODUCTION

Our aim for this book is to provide students, practitioners and academics with a resource that offers research informed and practical guide to achieving the early childhood graduate practitioner competencies (ECGPCs). We have drawn on experiences from higher education (HE) institutions who have significant experience embedding the ECGPCs alongside their Early Childhood Studies Degrees; as well as a detailed explanation of each competency, colleagues share examples from student portfolios. This introduction includes a brief history of the ECGPCs, advice on evidencing your ECGPCs, and explains how each contributor responds to the individual competencies.

BACKGROUND TO THE EARLY CHILDHOOD GRADUATE COMPETENCIES

Introduced in 2018, the competencies were created in response to ever changing government policy on the requirements for early childhood practitioners. The lack of understanding of the breadth of the early childhood workforce, which encompasses, health, education and care in all its manifestations led to a myopic assumption about the knowledge and skills needed for working in this complex sector. This view of a homogenous 'one size fits all' workforce led to a raft of government initiatives focused on education to the exclusion of holistic child centred policy and practice which differs across the four nations of the United Kingdom. Acknowledging the shifting policy landscape, the Early Childhood Studies Degrees Network (ECSDN) took the initiative and developed the Early Childhood Graduate Practitioner Competencies (ECGPCs), to 'afford students with placement opportunities to critically apply theory to practice in a range of early childhood settings and/or school, social care and health settings' (ECSDN, 2018, p. 7).

Creating the ECGPCs was driven by the need to offer our collective students the best learning opportunity in a focused way. The ECGPCs are now included in the Quality Assurance Agency Early Childhood Studies Benchmark Statement (QAA, 2022).

RATIONALE FOR THIS BOOK

This book responds to findings that emerged from research that sought the views of the ECEC sector about the introduction of the ECGPCs. Following the launch of the Competencies, the ECSDN created a funding opportunity for research to find out more about the early experiences of the people who were involved in the first cohorts of students to study for the competencies. Two teams of researchers were awarded funding to carry out projects.

The content of this book draws on the experiences of the graduate practitioners who participated in Fairchild et al. (2022) study. In particular, we highlight one of the main findings:

Those settings that employed graduates were able to know the important link between knowledge and professional practice. This research highlighted that reflective practice was an important component of the role where graduates knew the 'why' as well as the 'how'. (p 2)

We include case studies written by ECS students undertaking the ECGPCs that explicitly link theory, that is the 'why' with the practice, that is 'the how'. The students' case studies demonstrate the importance of their reflective stance as a critical ingredient in making the links between theory and practice. Richardson, Wall and Brogaard-Clausen (2022) in the second piece of ECSDN funded research found that there was a need for more support for students in how to evidence the competencies. They also found that there was a need for more examples of evidence to be shared. These points are illustrated by the following comment:

The competencies help to give the student a focus [...] When collecting evidence, the student can link the competencies specifically and give examples to show they have achieved them.

(Voice of a Mentor, in Richardson et al., 2022, p. 14)

The content of each chapter in this book will support students to see how they can prepare evidence for the competencies, as well as providing excellent exemplars in a focused and accessible way.

COLLECTING YOUR EVIDENCE

The content of this book will provide useful information for whatever area of the early childhood workforce you are working in or aiming to work in; as a graduate practitioner, you will be able to critically apply theory to practice in your work with babies, young children, families' carers.

You will notice as you progress through your degree and your placements that the competencies embrace all aspects of children's care learning and development. You may find it challenging to see where your evidence should sit. That is to be expected, you will begin recognising the holistic nature of the competencies. You will need to consider how you can cross reference your evidence, to show your understanding of the connections between the competencies, your practice and your academic study. Caitlin Armstrong, an Early Childhood Graduate Practitioner, offers her advice about how she approached the task of gathering evidence:

... I learnt that it would be helpful to carry post-it's with me to be able to instantly note anything that could go towards my evidence. I also wrote down all the competencies onto a set of revision cards that I kept handy so I could track across my evidence whenever I had some free time.

Caitlin Armstrong (Early Childhood Graduate Practitioner) The University of Sunderland

THEORETICAL FRAMEWORK

Early Childhood Studies degrees adopt an holistic approach to knowledge and understanding of the ecology of child development in the context of the family, community and wider socio-political contexts' (ECSDN, 2018, p. 4). Throughout the book, we draw on theory to frame the content; in particular, Urie Bronfenbrenner's (1979) ecological systems theory helps to explore the influence of different contexts on children's lives.

THE TERMS WE USE

We recognise that terminology in early childhood education and care can complex, each term has its own history and connections. With so many contributing authors, we have opted for consistency about the following terms and phrases:

EARLY CHILDHOOD EDUCATION AND CARE

Throughout the book we refer to the sector as ECEC. We use this term to include all aspects of the sector, where young children are educated and cared for. We are aware that others use terms such as 'childcare' 'early years' or 'early childhood education'. While we understand why they are in use we use ECEC because effective education for all children, but particularly for our youngest children, relies on all aspects of personal and interpersonal care.

EARLY CHILDHOOD GRADUATE PRACTITIONER

Early Childhood Graduate Practitioner refers to students working towards, or those who have completed the Early Childhood Graduate Practitioner Competencies.

OVERVIEW OF CHAPTERS

Although this book can be read from beginning to end, it is intended to be used as a resource to support you with ideas of how to evidence each individual competency. As well as a detailed explanation of each competency, the chapters feature examples of practice, ideas for evidence gathering, reflective questions, tasks and recommended reading. These points can be used to facilitate your reflection on the content and provide you with the opportunity to consider your own observations and critical interpretation of the ECGPCs.

In **Chapter 1**, David Meechan explores Competency 1: Advocating for young children's rights and participation. Student vignettes will evidence the development and application of knowledge, skills and practice, based on how listening, collaboration, and co-construction, not only underpins a rights-based approach for children but also ECS students and the future professionals in the sector.

Amanda Tayler, Tara Ball and Heather Brammer address Competency 2: Promote holistic child development in **Chapter 2**. Drawing on a range of theoretical perspectives, they offer detailed knowledge and understanding of child development, to equip you with (more) confidence, knowledge and understanding around how to care and educate children in the twenty-first century.

In **Chapter 3**, Aaron Bradbury and Jackie Musgrave examine Competency 3: Work directly with young children, families and colleagues to promote health, well-being, safety and nurturing care. This chapter focuses on factors that influence children's health, development and well-being. The content will foreground the vital role that ECEC settings contribute to supporting and promoting the health of babies and young children.

Selena Hal and Dawn Jones share their knowledge and experience regarding Competency 4: Observe, listen and plan for young children to support their well-being, early learning, progression and transitions in **Chapter 4**. They explore the process of understanding children through observing and listening as a developing professional, underpinned by reference to the Birth to 5 Matters theme of 'the unique child' in the 'everchanging context'. Three case studies independently written by students will share their placement experiences and how these experiences have assisted them to build upon and develop their early childhood graduate practitioner competency (ECGPC) evidence.

In **Chapter 5**, Caroline Prior tackles Competency 5: Safeguarding and child protection. She argues the fundamental principle of safeguarding involves adopting a child-centred approach that places a child's safety and best interests at the core of high-quality professional practice. Caroline explores the key principles of safeguarding and child protection from a practice stance, including how to understand the complex and multi-faceted components of child abuse and neglect in modern society and your role in working as part of a multi-disciplinary team.

In **Chapter 6**, Deborah Nye and Helen Perkins explore Competency 6: Inclusive practice. Chapter 6 unpick the concept of inclusive practice, through the lens of the 'Unique child'. The chapter considers the protected characteristics, identified in the Equality Act, 2010. Student case studies highlight the importance of representation for both children and their families. The discussion following each case study will assist you in building your knowledge and skills in terms of inclusive practice and the reflective questions will challenge you to consider your personal values and beliefs, and to develop your personal pedagogy.

Competency 7: Partnership with parents and caregivers is presented by Philippa Thompson. She examines the theory behind parent partnership in **Chapter 7**. Beginning by asking what is meant by partnership with parents and/or caregivers, Philippa provides an overview of government policy in England over the past 25 years. This policy is explored in the next part of the chapter to consider how policy plays a part in influencing practice. The next consideration are the differing perspectives of all those involved. The child, the parents and/or caregivers, students and practitioners and other professionals are all discussed. Finally, a case study and summary support the consideration of practice alongside research and policy for completion of this competency.

In **Chapter 8**, Leanne Grey and Michelle Wisbey address Competency 8: Collaborating with others. Underpinning daily life in an early childhood setting is the importance of creating successful, respectful and professional relationships with colleagues and other professionals both within and outside the setting. Working as a member of a team and in multi-professional contexts can result in challenges and barriers. However, collaborative working in practice, including effective listening, can reduce the impact of these challenges and barriers. In this chapter, Leanne and Michelle consider how ECGPC students can develop their understanding of collaborating with others in both a theoretical and practical context.

Finally, **Chapter 9** looks at Competency 9: Professional development. Meredith Rose, Stella Smith and Matthew Northall provide readers with a range of opportunities to reflect upon both theory and practice. The chapter will prompt a discussion about key concepts and explores the ever-changing influences on early childhood practices. The graduate journey relies upon an engagement with current literature and contemporary debates to become a critical and reflective practitioner. Case studies and reflections will help you recognise your expertise and plan for your personal CPD journey. Supporting the graduates to develop into confident and articulate practitioners are key themes, alongside the opportunities to be research active and engage in helping Early Childhood Studies evolve.

A final piece of advice from Caitlin:

I finalised my portfolio by tracking across all relevant assignments from the three years of my course and formatting>printing>filing>tracking all my evidence I had created.

My most important piece of advice to anyone completing the ECGPCs would be to stay organised. I followed a system that worked for me that allowed me to complete placement, create evidence, and keep track of which competencies I had met throughout (personally, I would keep notes throughout the placement day, type these into something more tangible once I got home, then finalise the piece of work within the same week so I didn't forget anything important).

THE EARLY CHILDHOOD GRADUATE COMPETENCIES: VISUAL SUMMARIES

1

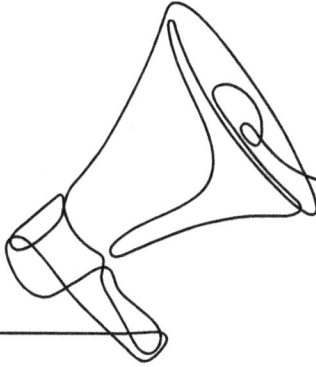

Advocating for young children's rights and participation

1.1 Demonstrate how you listen to and work in collaboration with young children, individually and in groups.

1.2 Observe, support and extend young children's participation in their learning through following their needs and interests.

1.3 Support children to respect others by providing opportunities for their participation and decision making.

2

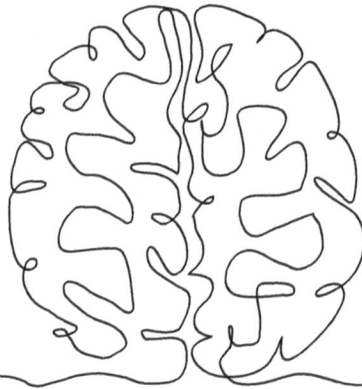

Promote holistic child development

2.1 Explain, justify and apply in practice, knowledge of how infants and young children develop from conception to the age of 8

2.2 Demonstrate and apply knowledge to practice of the factors that promote and impede holistic development and long-term outcomes.

3

Work directly with young children, families and colleagues to promote health, well-being, safety and nurturing care.

3.1 Explain what factors influence health and wellbeing.

3.2 Demonstrate the application of knowledge about health, well-being and safety to practice.

3.3 Apply data protection legislation to practice.

3.4 Know and demonstrate how to complete a risk assessment and apply in practice.

3.5 Understand factors which influence nutritional health and integrate knowledge about current dietary guidance into practice, including early feeding and weaning.

3.6 Demonstrate the application of knowledge and understanding about the importance of respectful nurturing care routines.

3.7 Demonstrate how to promote health and educate children and families about health-related matters.

4

Observe, listen and plan for young children to support their wellbeing, early learning, progression and transitions

4.1 Know and understand the relevant Early Childhood curriculum frameworks and apply them in practice.

4.2 Apply a range of observation and research skills to co-construct young children's development, play and learning, encouraging independence and next steps.

4.3 Evidence the application of different theoretical perspectives when planning for young children's personal, social and emotional development.

4.4 Apply theoretical understanding to the range of transitions young children experience and how these can be effectively supported in practice.

4.5 Evidence knowledge of the importance of parents and/or caregivers and the home learning environment in infants and young children's development and learning.

4.6 Demonstrate knowledge and skill in listening to and communicating verbally and non-verbally with children and how to encourage their communication skills,

4.7 Identify and apply pedagogical knowledge of how to develop enabling environments indoors and outdoors.

4.8 Explain and demonstrate understanding of the balance between child-led and adult-led activities.

4.9 Using real world contexts apply to practice theoretical understanding of Language development; Literacy development (including early reading and writing) and Mathematical concepts.

4.10 Evidence contemporary knowledge and skills in the use of technology and the role and appropriate use of digital literacies in young children's learning.

4.11 Enable young children to understand the wider world.

5

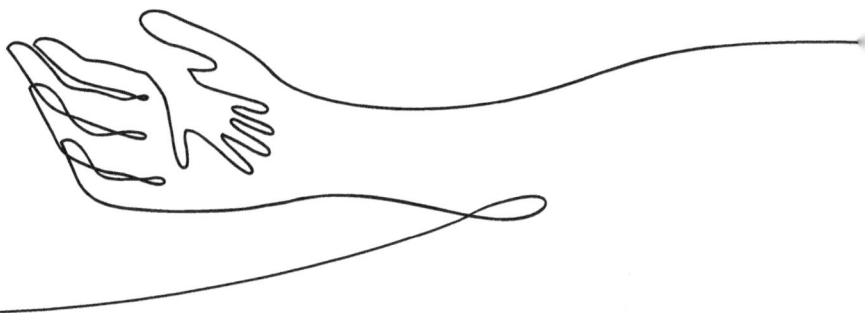

Safeguarding and child protection

5.1 Know the wider legislative and statutory guidance for safeguarding including child protection, whistle blowing, digital safety and how these are articulated into setting policy.

5.2 Recognise when a child may be in danger or at risk of serious harm and the procedures that must be followed.

5.3 Appreciate the importance of working with others to safeguard and promote the well-being of infants and young children.

5.4 Evidence advanced knowledge about child abuse, the wider theoretical perspectives about the causes of abuse and the potential implications for young children's outcomes.

5.5 Apply knowledge of adverse childhood experience, including child abuse to individual planning.

5.6 Evidence and apply knowledge and understanding of how globalisation and technology may pose safeguarding risks for young children.

5.7 Know when to signpost to other services or designated persons within the setting to secure young children's safeguarding and protection.

6

Inclusive practice

6.1 Evidence knowledge, understanding and application in practice of pedagogy that supports inclusion.

6.2 Know how to identify infants and young children who may require additional support and how to refer to appropriate services.

6.3 Demonstrate an understanding of statutory guidance for children with Special Educational Needs and Disabilities and Protected Characteristics.

6.4 Evidence skills in appropriate planning to address the care and early learning needs of individual young children with special educational needs and/or disabilities and Protected Characteristics.

7

Partnership with parents and caregivers

7.1 Evidence understanding of the importance of partnership with parents and/or caregivers in their role as infants and young children's first educators.

7.2 Demonstrate in practice the co-construction of learning in respectful partnership with parents and/or caregivers.

7.3 Apply knowledge to practice, about the diversity of family life and society.

7.4 Demonstrate skills in communicating and working in partnership with families.

8

Collaborating with others

8.1 Evidence knowledge about the importance of creating successful, respectful professional relationships with colleagues and other professionals in and outside the setting.

8.2 Apply collaborative skills in practice, including effective listening and working as a member of a team and in multi-professional contexts.

8.3 Demonstrate an understanding of the barriers to working with others and how to address these in practice.

9

Professional development

9.1 Demonstrate self-awareness and knowledge of anti-discriminatory practice, promoting social justice and the importance of valuing difference, including gender, ethnicity, religious affiliation and sexual orientation.

9.2 Evidence skills in enabling the voice of young children to be heard. 9.3 Evidence advanced skills in utilising reflective practice alongside research, to enhance your continual professional development in Early Childhood.

9.3 Draw on research to demonstrate knowledge of leadership and management and its importance and application in democratic and inclusive practice. 9.5 Recognise and evidence the importance of communicating effectively orally and in writing to others.

1

ADVOCATING FOR YOUNG CHILDREN'S RIGHTS AND PARTICIPATION

David Meechan

CHAPTER ACKNOWLEDGEMENTS

With thanks to the following students and practitioners for their contributions:
Lianne Tetsell – Early Childhood Studies Student
Lisa Whitehouse – Early Years Setting Leader
Helen Lloyd – Practice Educator

By the end of this chapter, you will be able to:

- Articulate what advocacy means and why it is important for children.
- Understand some of the factors that contribute to promoting children's rights and participation in practice.
- Consider what types of evidence you can collect for Competency 1.
- Reflect on your own experiences and make connections between your studies and placement.

KEY TERMS AND DEFINITIONS INCLUDED IN THIS CHAPTER

Children's rights	This relates to the United Nations Convention on the Rights of a Child (UNCRC) in 1989. The UNCRC includes 54 articles which details how children should be treated and how adults and governments should work together to ensure this happens.
Advocacy	This means getting support from other people, professionals, organisations and the government to fulfil children's rights.
Participation	This is more than just allowing children to take part; it is also planning for children to take part and enabling them to direct their participation.

INTRODUCTION

This chapter will begin by discussing the different aspects of Early Childhood Graduate Practitioner Competency (ECGPC) 1: advocacy, children's rights and participation.

COMPETENCY 1: ADVOCATING FOR YOUNG CHILDREN'S RIGHTS AND PARTICIPATION

1.1   Demonstrate how you listen to and work in collaboration with young children, individually and in groups.

1.2   Observe, support and extend young children's participation in their learning through following their needs and interests.

1.3   Support children to respect others by providing opportunities for their participation and decision-making.

This chapter presents several case studies. The first case study presents the insights of a level 5 student undertaking an Early Childhood Studies (ECS) degree. The student has shared an experience from placement and demonstrates how placement can help you to achieve GPC 1. The second case study presents the insights of a leader from an early years setting and an example of what level 6 practice involves when considering children's rights in day-to-day decisions. The final case study presents the insights of a practice educator from the University of Wolverhampton whose role it is to visit, support and assess ECS students undertaking the ECGPCs. Following each case study is a discussion and reflection of how it may be linked to the different evidence points of Competency 1. There is then a section recognising the wider dimensions of Competency 1 which are not addressed in the case studies. Finally, a summary of the chapter is provided with reflective questions.

There are three key aspects to consider for Competency 1: advocacy, children's rights and participation.

ADVOCACY

Competency 1 can be divided into three aspects. The first aspect is advocacy. Advocating for young children, families and the Early Years workforce is essential if we are to improve the experiences and outcomes for children in our society (Thomas et al., 2017). Advocacy for children can be traced back to over 100 years ago in the United Kingdom, when Eglantyne Webb founded Save the Children in 1919. There are prominent organisations and networks that advocate for many things related to the early years sector in the United Kingdom. Examples include the Early Years Alliance, the National Children's Bureau, Family Action, the Children's Society, Action for Healthy Kids and the Care Workers Charity. These organisations advocate for a range of improvements to be made regarding policy and legislation. Advocacy, however, also takes place on a day-to-day basis. In fact, it is advocating for the children and families that you work with as a professional which is the essential cornerstone of this competency. During your

ECS degree you will explore cross-cutting themes that enable you to develop your advocacy skills such as:

- equality, diversity and inclusion
- education for sustainable development
- entrepreneurship and enterprise education

(QAA, 2022, p. 1)

Advocacy can take several forms but in terms of early childhood practice; Urie Bronfenbrenner has summed it up best: 'Somebody's got to be crazy about that kid, and vice versa!' (Bronfenbrenner, 1990, p. 32). This means that as a professional you will be able to promote or advocate for the best interests of the children and families that you work with and back it up. In this sense, you will bring an informed rationality (knowledge and skills) to the cause. The big question next is how do you know what the best interests of a child are? This ultimately refers to supporting a child's needs relating to their health, well-being and development. This is where the second aspect of this competency gives you further guidance in terms of children's rights (Murray, Swadener and Smith, 2019).

CHILDREN'S RIGHTS

Discussion of children's rights is predominant across Early Childhood Studies degrees with reference to the United Nations Convention on the Rights of the Child (UN CRC, 1989). However, such predominance is not always reflected in the language and dialogue used in settings where students undertake placements. This is by no means to say that settings do not consider children's rights, but to highlight that discussion regarding the rights of children may not be as overt or obvious as presented on an ECS degree as it is in practice. Early childhood is also an area of devolved governance for the four countries of the United Kingdom, meaning that each country has different frameworks that influence practice and the language used. For example, there is no direct mention of children's rights in England's statutory or non-statutory guidance for the Early Years Foundation Stage (DfE, 2021a, 2021b). However, in England, an alternative non-statutory guide for the Early Years Foundation Stage called Birth to 5 Matters (Early Years Coalition, 2021) refers to children's rights throughout. Furthermore, the national guidance for Pre-Birth to Three in Scotland (Learning and Teaching Scotland, 2010, p. 19), the Rights of the Child are considered as the first of four key principles and underpin the framework.

As an early childhood student completing the ECGPCs, your challenge is to make connections between the day-to-day practice on placement with the modules you undertake at university, relating this to the ECGPCs. You do have several years to practice and develop your understanding of children's rights across your study though, so please do not panic! Embedding children's rights in practice is known as a rights-based approach to practice and was explored during the Children's Parliament's (2021) Year of Childhood. Furthermore, an essential part of rights-based practice in early years is the concept of participation. The following activity supports you in reflecting on how you encourage children to participate.

REFLECTION

CHILDREN'S RIGHTS IN CURRICULUM FRAMEWORKS

As mentioned in this chapter, some curriculum frameworks and guidance relating to early childhood directly reference and cite children's rights, but other frameworks do not. This does not mean that the latter frameworks object to children's rights, but that the connections are not made explicit. Please choose the curriculum framework that is most relevant to your studies and consider how the following articles of the UNCRC may be addressed through practice:

- How are children's views, feelings and wishes respected in all matters affecting them? (Article 12)
- How are children encouraged to express themselves? (Article 13)
- How are children's beliefs, thoughts and religion respected? (Article 14)
- How are children encouraged to associate with one another constructively? (Article 15)

PARTICIPATION

As you progress in your studies and placement experiences, you will become increasingly aware of the complexities behind participation when considering children. Your developing understanding of pedagogy and how children can be supported to learn and develop will mean questioning aspects of practice that you have not questioned before. For example, can children access other resources than those set out? Can children choose where to sit at carpet time? Can children serve themselves at lunchtime? These questions reflect on the extent to which children make decisions about the experiences they have instead of having such decisions made for them. In terms of children's rights, it is encouraging their participation. Participation is one of the 'three Ps' that underpin a rights-based approach to practice, with the other two Ps being provision and protection (Livingstone, 2016). Theoretical models have also been developed to aid reflection and planning for children's participation. Hart's (1992) ladder of participation is one of the better-known models that distinguishes between non-participation and degrees of participation. Such a model can both inform and support reflections on practice. The Scottish Childminders Association (2016) have also produced a guide on 'Child-led participation' which expands on Hart's ladder of participation and applies it to practical examples. Shier (2001) presents a model for enhancing children's involvement with decision-making in line with the UNCRC (1989). This is called 'Pathways to Participation', which involves five levels with each level considering openings, opportunities and obligations. Ultimately, what this competency is concerned with is that you are a vocal advocate for children based on their rights and know how to support children's participation within your professionalism (Figure 1.1).

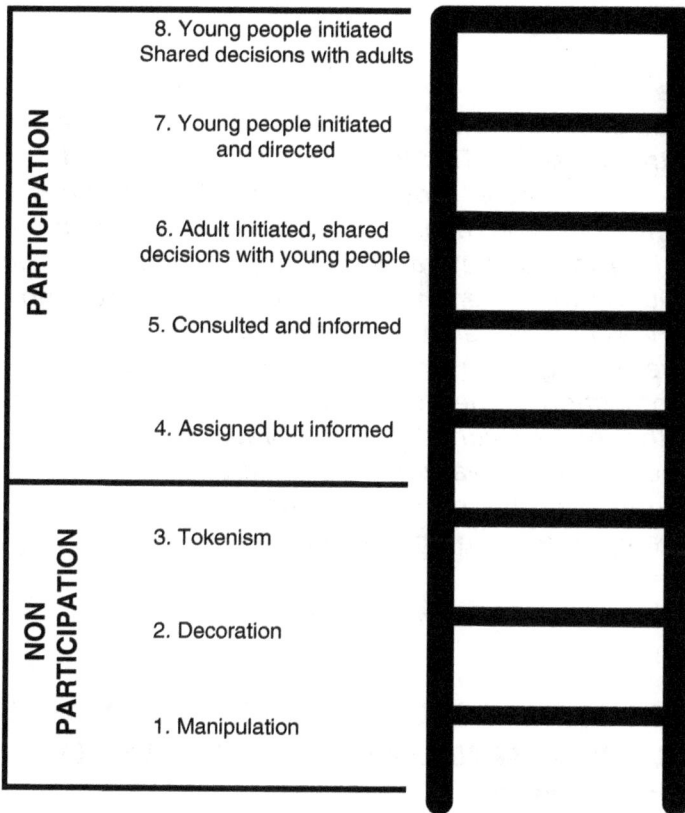

Figure 1.1 Roger Hart's ladder of children's participation
Source: Adapted From Hart, R. (1992) Childrens Participation: From tokenism to citizenship, Florence, UNICEF International Child Development Centre.

CASE STUDY 1: INSIGHTS FROM A LEVEL 5 ECS STUDENT

Advocating for children's rights and participation is in everything I do now I know what they are. This means ensuring children consistently have opportunities to be included and participate throughout the day. This means being responsive to children's needs and behaviours in order to allow them to access opportunities within the learning environment. For example, where I am on placement, I have been working with a boy who is non-verbal and has displayed autistic spectrum disorder traits (although awaiting a diagnosis). He lacks self-control at times, and this can lead to head banging and other potentially harmful behaviours. A fellow practitioner had asked him not to do something and he became visibly upset. I was asked to take him to the next room to help him calm down. After trying numerous strategies, I

(Continued)

(Continued)

found that massaging his feet worked best and helped defuse some of the tension that had built up. However, when returning to the room, he began to get visibly distressed again. This time, massaging his feet did not work, so I began to play a game where I would crawl up to him and bang the floor with my hands, before tickling him. This distracted him from the anxiety of returning to the room as he was visibly enjoying the game and began to really laugh. During this time, I had also been using some simple signs being aware that he was non-verbal. After a while, a practitioner entered the room to see how we were getting on, and while I stopped playing the game to speak to the practitioner, the boy came to me and signed 'more'. This was the first time that he had signed, and the practitioner informed me that this was one of the targets he was working towards. Shortly after, the boy was ready to return to the other room where he could engage with the learning opportunities and other children once more.

COMMENTARY ON CASE STUDY 1 IN RELATION TO 1.1 DEMONSTRATE HOW YOU LISTEN TO AND WORK IN COLLABORATION WITH YOUNG CHILDREN, INDIVIDUALLY AND IN GROUPS

The student in Case Study 1 is demonstrating active **listening** through responding to the child's needs. For example, the child shows distress twice in the example and the student moves to address this. First and foremost, it is not in the best interests of a child to be regularly distressed. Both times the student responds to this by calming down the child. These actions and attempts are aimed at supporting the child to return to a state where they can regulate their behaviour. Initially, this is through co-regulation and then self-regulation. This is important as unless the child is able to self-regulate, then their behaviours may not only impede their own opportunities for learning but also those of other children. In this context, the student's actions are supporting both the **individual** child as well as the wider **group** of children to have access to their entitled learning experiences. The student is not only advocating for this child to be included, but they demonstrate perseverance by not giving up and attempting multiple strategies to help the child regulate. Ultimately, they are advocating for this child to be included so that they can participate. Both strategies used by the student, such as massaging the child's feet and then playing the game, demonstrate attempts to encourage **collaboration** with the child. This climaxes in the non-verbal child communicating through signing 'more' when the student stops playing the game. Wider consideration can be given to the child's right to access and participate in the day-to-day activities offered if they are removed from the room. However, had the child not had the time and space away from the initial trigger of not being able to do what he wanted, then he could have potentially spiralled into certain behaviours both dangerous for himself and other children. Responding to his needs after the initial trigger and in the other room helped smooth the transition back into the environment with his peers.

HOW DO I RECORD EVIDENCE FOR MY PORTFOLIO?

Reflecting on your practice experience is a key aspect of developing your knowledge and experiences in order to achieve the ECGPCs. To do this, it is important that you evidence your own journey throughout your studies. If you were the student in Case Study 1, this could be recorded and evidenced in several ways. Depending on your university's guidance, it could be recorded as a **reflective account**. Remember, at level 6, reflective accounts need to go further than description to include synthesis with wider literature and policy in relation to practice. This will mean that the reflective account is a critical reflection. You may also be able to ask a practitioner to provide a **witness statement** in support of such an experience. But again, being able to critically articulate why this is of importance to GPC 1 is what will be needed to support you in your final viva. Look back at the words in bold to see where Case Study 1 is explored in direct relation to GPC 1.

CASE STUDY 2: INSIGHTS FROM A LEADER OF AN EARLY YEARS SETTING

I believe that a level 6 practitioner should have the knowledge and professionalism to be a critical friend when considering the rights of children in practice, policy and leadership. This means understanding context and issues beyond day-to-day practice and can often involve creatively stretching the resources and opportunities presented. By doing this, statutory requirements should not only be met but exceeded. Such examples will impact positively on the practice of others. For example, when we introduced a free-flow policy between the 2–3-year-old room and the outside area, it became apparent that the free-flow opportunity was being stopped during the time that practitioners took their lunch breaks. Therefore, the children only had access to free-flow provision for reduced periods in the morning and afternoon. Children are at the centre of any decisions we make, so I asked the senior room leader to reflect with their team on why free-flow provision was not being maximised throughout the day.

Initially, the team raised valid concerns relating to ratios. This was because when several practitioners were on lunch at once, they would not be in ratio, should the remaining practitioners be split between the outside and inside environment. The senior room leader challenged the team on this though, as children had responded really positively to the free-flow arrangements. The team had observed heightened levels of engagement and concentration as children were able to decide where, how and when they would access resources and move freely between inside and outside. In essence, the senior room leader was reminding the team to put the children at the centre of the discussion, and that children should have a categorical right to choose where

(Continued)

(Continued)

and how they play which is supported by routine. If lunch breaks are, therefore, disrupting free-flow access for the children, then what steps can be taken as practitioners to address this? With these prompts, the team decided to reduce the number of practitioners on lunch break at one time as this would enable ratios to be met during free flow, maximising the opportunities for children to freely direct and choose how they played. This final decision to put the children's best interests first and be able to justify this in terms of supporting a child's right to play demonstrates how children's rights are embedded in the strategic as well as operational decisions of running our setting.

COMMENTARY ON CASE STUDY 2 IN RELATION TO 1.2 OBSERVE, SUPPORT AND EXTEND YOUNG CHILDREN'S PARTICIPATION IN THEIR LEARNING THROUGH FOLLOWING THEIR NEEDS AND INTERESTS

The insights from the setting leader demonstrate the expectations of a graduate in terms of knowledge, skills and essentially practice wisdom which stems beyond the statutory requirements. Achieving the ECGPCs will mean that you are a knowledgeable, skilled and a competent practitioner who can lead others. The senior room leader in the example above is tasked with acknowledging practitioner concerns relating to ratios, but also to work with their team to find a solution that keeps the best interests of the children central. Once the concern around ratios was acknowledged, the reminder of what had been **observed**, and was working really well in terms of **supporting children's participation** in their learning environment was raised regarding access to free-flow provision. Furthermore, the intervention from the setting leader via the senior room leader is an example of a professional advocating for children's best interests in terms of their opportunities to play. Through joint discussion, a democratic solution is reached that demonstrates the team's professionalism in making changes to how/when lunch breaks are taken. These changes accommodate free-flow provision throughout the day in recognition of the **children's needs and interests**. As a student on placement, you may not have the opportunity to be involved in such discussions. However, what is important is that you are inquisitive and ask the 'why' question around practice and routines. Especially if changes are made while you are there or if you see areas where potential changes could impact positively on practice. By level 6, you should be familiar with considering the intent, implementation and impact (Ofsted, 2022) of decisions that support children as individuals to access their rights. If you undertake a university module that asks you to consider making/leading a change at the setting, then this is a great opportunity to work with your placement and support them to make a meaningful change. Such an assignment could also be used as evidence towards this competency. Remember that advocating for children's rights and encouraging participation should be as evident in the policies of a setting as it is in practice.

CASE STUDY 3 – INSIGHTS FROM A PRACTICE EDUCATOR AT THE UNIVERSITY OF WOLVERHAMPTON

Students will be taught about children's rights on their ECS programme. For students to be able to evidence a good understanding of Competency 1 at the end point assessment at level 6, they must be able to make links between their learning as part of the degree at university and their learning on placement. Sometimes the degree will cover aspects of childhood that are new or unfamiliar to students as well as present alternative ways of supporting children's development. The aim of this is to prepare students for being a professional and having the confidence to address, reflect and potentially challenge certain situations in the future. Working across age groups students may experience different pedagogical approaches. Such opportunities allow students to develop their own values and inform their approaches to working with children and families as a professional.

On a visit to a student in a Year 1 class I observed a holding activity before registration that involved children sitting at their desks to complete a subtraction activity with certain children being given fidget spinners to aid concentration. During feedback and discussion after the observation, it became clear that the student was quite disheartened about being given such an activity to deliver for the observation. This was because the activity lacked any elements of play or child centredness. The student clearly articulated that should they have been allowed to plan the activity, it would have been play-based and differentiated to incorporate the range of interests and abilities of the children in the group. The student explained that their rationale for this related to the international perspectives that had been covered in sessions as part of their ECS degree. The student did not feel able to influence the observed session, but such a strong reflection demonstrated the student's understanding and how they valued the individual children in class and respected their differences to aid learning. Allowing children the opportunity to engage in a subtraction activity via a play-based approach would increase participation and children's ownership over how they engaged with the concept of subtraction. This, in turn, may have just minimised the need for fidget spinners or bums on seats in a pre-registration activity!

COMMENTARY ON CASE STUDY 3 IN RELATION TO 1.3 SUPPORT CHILDREN TO RESPECT OTHERS BY PROVIDING OPPORTUNITIES FOR THEIR PARTICIPATION AND DECISION MAKING

A core part of supporting children to respect each other is respecting them first and foremost. The above insight provides a window into the opposing pedagogies that can be experienced by children as they move from the EYFS to the National Curriculum framework in England through the eyes of an ECS student. The real learning evidenced here towards Competency 1 is that there are different ways of **providing opportunities for children's participation** and **decision-making**. Fundamentally, the desk-based, adult overseen activity observed seems to have minimalised participation and missed opportunities that would support children's learning and development fully. Although the activity was focussed on subtraction, allowing children to select their own resources and negotiate this with other children through a play-based approach would open up new learning opportunities. An example of such opportunities is the concept of sharing and negotiation, something that from my experience can need regular guidance. However, it does not need a commitment of forcing children to share whenever they are asked to. For example, a child may have gathered their favourite classroom items and be counting, building up to practising subtraction when another child takes one item and tells the child that it is okay because they are sharing. In such circumstances, children will need to be **supported to respect** each other through dialogue. Providing a narration of the events for both children to listen to, before returning the taken item to the original child and redirecting the other child's attention to alternative resources that can be used instead would be a professional approach. Through modelling and facilitating such exchanges, the ethos of children respecting each other as individuals will be promoted.

ADVOCATING FOR YOUNG CHILDREN'S RIGHTS AND PARTICIPATION: CONSIDERATIONS OF THE WIDER CONTEXT AND IMPACT ON PRACTICE AND PROVISION

The three case studies have provided examples relating to Competency 1. It is important to highlight that these are only snapshots within the scope of Competency 1, and that there are many factors relating to children's rights and practice that warrant further consideration. These factors exist at different levels within the child's environment, at the individual, family, community and society level which interact in complex ways. The following diagram Figure 1.2 has been adapted from a model provided by the Early Intervention Foundation:

REFLECTION

- What modules have you studied on your degree that relate to children's rights? What were your key take away points from these?
- From placement experience, can you think of examples where your practice has actively supported children to participate?
- Consider how you can synthesise (connect) the learning from university with your placement experiences in terms of advocacy, children's rights and participation?
- Identify three experiences from placement and study that you could use as evidence towards this competency. What links are there between literature, this competency and your experience? How will you evidence and justify this process in your portfolio?

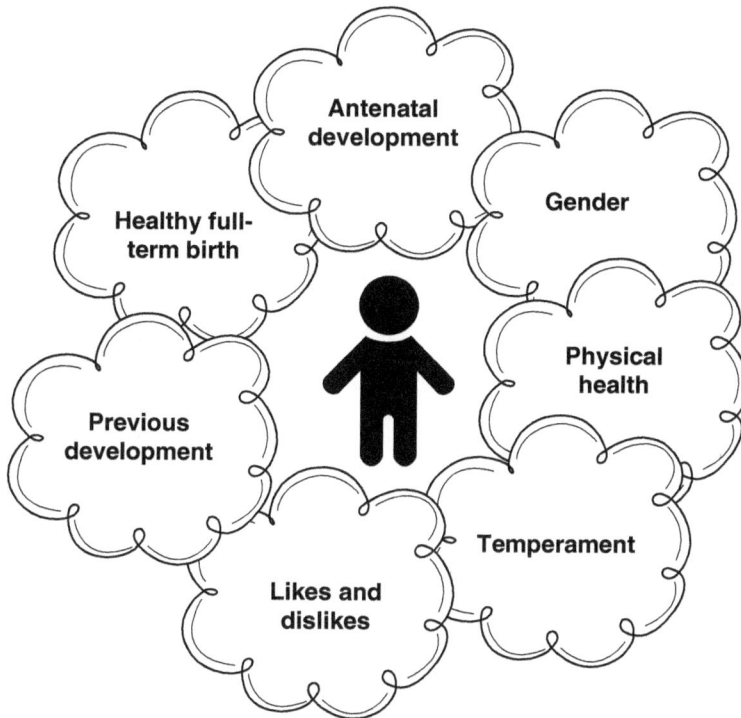

Figure 1.2 Children's environments and the factors affecting them
(Diagram is for illustration purposes, and there are many other factors including the family and the child's community).

CHAPTER SUMMARY

This chapter has introduced Competency 1 by discussing its three core aspects: advocacy, children's rights and participation. Although advocacy can be undertaken at the government and policy level, Competency 1 is concerned with students advocating for children through daily practice and the decisions made that inform practice. The setting leader in Case Study 2 is highlighted as advocating for children's right to play in their setting and ensuring that routines support this. The second aspect discussed is with reference to children's rights themselves, the difference in the devolved nations of the United Kingdom's Early Years frameworks and a rights-based approach to practice. A rights-based approach also involves putting children at the centre of all decisions, and this can be seen throughout the three case studies presented, that children's needs and best interests are kept central to the discussion. The third aspect considered was participation which is known as one of the fundamental 3 Ps, of a rights-based approach, with the other two Ps being provision and protection. Both students in Case Studies 1 and 3 promote the participation of children in their practice. While in Case Study 1, the student supports the child to regulate in order to participate, the student in Case Study 3 recognises and critiques the lack of children's participation in the activity that they were asked to deliver.

The three case studies were chosen to demonstrate the breadth of experience that can be drawn on to support students in developing their portfolios and confidence in this competency in order to achieve it at level 6. Ensuring that children's rights are considered and embedded is not only important for day-to-day practice as in Case Study 1 but also in strategic considerations such as in Case Study 2.

FURTHER READING

Arnott, L. and Wall, K. (2022) *The Theory and Practice of Voice in Early Childhood.* London: Routledge.

Correia, N., Aguiar, C., and Amaro, F. (2021) Children's participation in early childhood education: A theoretical overview. *Contemporary Issues in Early Childhood.* https://doi.org/10.1177/1463949120981789

McFarlane-Edmond, P. and Withers, C. (2023) *Effective Practice in the Early Years.* London: Sage Publishing.

2

PROMOTE HOLISTIC CHILD DEVELOPMENT

Tara Ball, Heather Brammer and *Amanda Tayler*

By the end of this chapter, you will be able to:

• Explore the factors which influence and impact on children's development.
• Demonstrate the application of knowledge about promoting and supporting children's holistic development and children who are hospitalised, including how these relate to your graduate practitioner competencies.
• Engage in the literature which supports the need for a robust and critical knowledge of child development and caring for sick children.
• Demonstrate the ability to apply theory to early childhood practice while gathering evidence for your graduate practitioner competencies.
• Develop an ongoing dialogue of practice and theoretical concepts to gain graduate knowledge and continual understandings of what holistic development means.

KEY TERMS AND DEFINITIONS INCLUDED IN THIS CHAPTER

Holistic Development	Holistic development means developing the whole child. The five aspects of holistic development are physical, intellectual, social, emotional and spiritual development
Bioecological System	A concept around the complexities of relationships and how a child develops
Hospitalised Children	Children who are admitted to hospital and have to stay overnight (or longer) because they are poorly/have a condition/undergoing treatments/procedures
Hospital Play Specialist	A specialised role and one which is educated in the care and recovery of children in hospital

INTRODUCTION

This chapter will focus on child development and how Competency 2 provides a foundation on which to support, promote and facilitate the holistic development of children.

COMPETENCY 2

2.1 Explain, justify and apply in practice knowledge of how infants and young children develop from conception to the age of 8 in terms of:
- neurological and brain development
- cognitive development
- communication and language development
- personal, emotional and social development
- physical development

2.2 Demonstrate and apply knowledge to practice of the factors that promote and impede holistic development and long-term outcomes. These include:
- individual circumstances
- family circumstances
- attachment
- physical health
- mental health
- personal, social and emotional well-being
- the impact of disadvantage and adverse childhood experiences
- relationships with friends and adults
- the importance of learning through play
- the role of creativity
- policy

Two (separate) real-life case studies from an education setting and a hospital will be used to support your understanding of Competency 2 with reference to how children's development is affected by hospitalisation. There will be a focus around unpicking theoretical perspectives including Bronfenbrenner's (1989) about a child's holistic development and the implications for practice.

HOLISTIC DEVELOPMENT

Holistic development emphasises the importance of the physical, emotional and psychological well-being of children. Children are unique and holistic learners who thrive in nurturing environments that support their 'individual and diverse motivations, interests and needs' (Early Years Coalition, 2021, p. 34). Each child's development and learning are comprised of numerous components; hence, an inclusive perspective around children's growth and development which later influence professional decisions is needed (Murphy, 2022).

Read the case study below and consider how the practitioner, Tania, supports the children's holistic development. Tania explores holistic development in the case study below.

CASE STUDY 1: TANIA

Tania was supervising a group of children in the natural area of the outside environment. The children were playing on the grass and then went over to watch some butterflies that had landed on the wildflowers planted in the small nature reserve. Tania went over to them and started to question what they could see which encouraged the children to look even more closely on the ground. Ben shouted that he could see 'bugs', and Sarah told everyone 'There's lots of creepy crawlies around.'

The children were enthralled, each one pointing out what insect they could see and describing it to their peers. Tania praised the children for being 'such careful watchers'. Tania asked the children 'Where do these insects go at night?' which led to a discussion about 'bug houses'. Tania suggested that together maybe they could create a bug shelter for when it got cold and dark. The children started to eagerly look around and began collecting twigs and leaves, sharing their ideas on how to build the shelter.

REFLECTION

Consider the following if you were supporting the children with the above activity:

- How are you encouraging the children to work together?
- How are you supporting the children's holistic development?
- How do you develop your understanding of each unique child to support their learning and development?
- How do you learn about each child's knowledge, strengths, ideas, abilities, interests?

COMMENTARY ON CASE STUDY 1

After completing your case study and reflective questions, you should consider the Graduate Practitioner Competence 2 and learn how this connects to practice. If you did something similar, what could you collect to link to your portfolio of evidence?

Here are some suggestions:

- Physical development: moving in the outdoor environment, fine motor skills such as moving twigs, leaves.
- Personal, social and emotional well-being and building relationships: the children are confident to engage with their peers, voicing their own ideas and considering each other's viewpoints, a sense of achievement after the shelters are complete.
- Cognitive: working in a group: using natural materials around them to build a shelter, explaining it to peers.
- Learning through play: During the activity the children practiced their movement and balancing skills, experimented with different moves and encouraged one another. They shared their ideas of moving along the lines, understanding each other through social interaction and are developing movement and balance understanding and respectful relationships.

SO WHY IS LEARNING ABOUT CHILD DEVELOPMENT SO IMPORTANT?

During a child's first few years of life, significant physical, social, cognitive and emotional development occurs. Young children discover who they are and how they fit into the world during their formative years. They are members of a group, whether it be a family, a community or a larger society. They are also a unique individual who develops and learns in a unique way (Brodie, 2018; Early Years Coalition, 2021). Observing and analysing children helps us understand the factors that contribute to their growth and development, laying the foundation for future development (Musgrave and Stobbs, 2015). By observing how children develop, we can understand why some children have difficulties and delays, as well as how to help them overcome hurdles and the actions to take. We can also better grasp how a child's physical, emotional and psychological development is affected by the environment. Therefore, it's crucial for practitioners, like you, to understand child development and each unique child. According to the revised EYFS Statutory framework, 'Every child is a unique child who is constantly learning and can be resilient, capable, confident and self-assured' (DfE, 2021, p. 6). Every child develops in a unique way, and growth is not a linear or automatic process. It depends on how each child can interact in positive relationships and enabling environments that foster engagement and recognise their strengths (Early Years Coalition, 2021).

REFLECTION

1. How and who decides children's daily experiences and routines?
2. How do you apply your knowledge of learning and development, and how does this affect children?
3. How do you critically reflect on pedagogy to provide quality learning experiences?

To find out more about theories of child development read Saracho's (2021) journal article 'Theories of Child development and their impact on Early Childhood Education and Care'.

As each child develops at their own rate, it is critical to take a holistic, professionally informed approach to developing an insightful understanding of a child's development to effectively plan for their individual learning requirements (Gov.UK, 2022; Pascal, Bertram and Rouse, 2019; Nutbrown, Clough and Atherton, 2013). A holistic summary considers not only the child's knowledge and skills but also the child's emotional well-being and connections, and learning attitudes and dispositions (Characteristics of Effective Learning) (Early Years Coalition, 2021; Murphy, 2022). Therefore, it is imperative that as an early years practitioner you are flexible, responsive and closely attuned with the children in your care.

Holistic development (Figure 2.1) below encompasses several domains.

Although it is useful to make distinctions between these domains (see Figure 2.1) (which will be discussed in the following sections), it is equally important to understand that they continually interact with each other.

Learning, growth and development of young children are interrelated and concurrent from birth (Brodie, 2018). By understanding holistic child development, you can be a more effective early years practitioner, develop a holistic approach, make informed and effective assessments, provide relevant and meaningful play opportunities to support each child's learning and development and develop effective parent partnerships by sharing information and guidance about their child's development and learning (Meggit, Bruce and Manning-Morton, 2016). Holistic development in Early Childhood Education and Care (ECEC) enables children to engage with their surroundings and learn, discover and explore in a unique way (Musgrave and Stobbs, 2015). Holistic development allows you to turn a child's favourite everyday activity into a learning opportunity, developing numerous aspects simultaneously. It enables you to plan since you know the children's interests, which boosts their learning, development and well-being. It increases children's curiosity and encourages them to study freely and creatively (Chilvers, 2018).

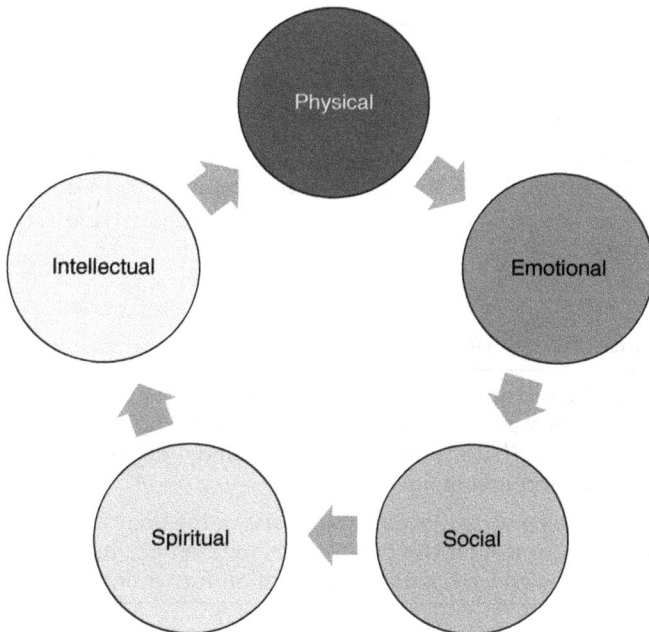

Figure 2.1 Holistic domains

In the United Kingdom, holistic child development is viewed as where every area of learning, development and growth is intertwined (Brodie, 2018; Whitebread and Coltman, 2015). Other countries share this view. For example, Nordic countries such as Denmark adopt a holistic perspective and objective where learning opportunities for each child are based on their individual needs with the concept that 'one size does not fit all' being a central premise of pedagogical approaches and practices (Wall, Litjens and Taguma, 2015). In addition, New Zealand's Te Whariki curriculum promotes holistic, continuous development from birth to starting school age with the focus on building individual children's strengths and interests within a socio-cultural and holistic approach and where the notions of being, belonging and becoming are all interconnected (Pascal, Bertram and Rouse, 2019).

PHYSICAL DEVELOPMENT

Physical development is a prime area and underpins all other areas of a young child's learning and development, enabling them to pursue happy, healthy and active lives (DfE, 2021; Meggit, Bruce and Manning-Morton, 2016). It includes the biological changes that occur in the body, such as changes in size and strength, integration of sensory and motor activities and increasing skill and functioning of the body. Movement and exercise is important for general health, and will help to increase circulation of blood in the body to help the child's brain to work actively (Bradbury and Swailes, 2022; Doherty and Hughes, 2014). When the brain, body and mind are viewed as one system, the effects of active physical play, health and self-care are observed, and the effects of adverse childhood experiences such as malnutrition, illness or neglect on a child's early brain development and mental health are recognised (Early Years Coalition, 2021).

Motor skills are the motions that are carried out when the brain, nervous system and muscles work together and can be split into two categories: gross and fine (see Table 2.1).

SOCIAL AND EMOTIONAL DEVELOPMENT

All children are unique and will develop socially and emotionally in different ways. Emotional development is the development of the ability to recognise, express (verbally and non-verbally) and manage feelings, as well as the ability to empathise with the feelings of others. The acquisition of the knowledge and skills required to interact with other children and adults and to form positive and rewarding relationships is referred to as social development (Neaum, 2022).

Table 2.1   Gross and fine motor skills

Gross motor skills	Involve the use of large muscles and body parts, like the arms and legs and include bigger movements, for example walking, jumping, balancing, dancing, running and climbing. These skills provide the foundation for developing healthy bodies and social and emotional well-being
Fine motor skills	Involve small muscle movements in parts of the body like the fingers, toes and feet and include small, precise movements, for example, using cutlery, writing or tying up shoelaces which builds the foundation for writing and drawing

Social and emotional development includes:

- The ability to express and understand emotions
- The ability to form caring and secure relationships
- The possibility to experience life in a positive and healthy way
- The development of emotional well-being

(Charlesworth, 2016)

This aspect of development naturally begins from the time a baby is born. A holistic, relational approach facilitates an environment conducive to trusting relationships, allowing children to engage with activities alone and with others, which fosters the development of friendships. By drawing on their own emotional awareness and collaborating with families to build mutually respectful, warm, welcoming connections with each of their key children, allows practitioners to meet the emotional needs of the children in their care (Cazaly, 2022; Early Years Coalition, 2021; Musgrave, 2017).

SPIRITUAL AND MORAL DEVELOPMENT

Moral and spiritual development consists of becoming aware of how to relate to others in an ethical, moral and humane manner. It does not require the formation of a particular faith; but it does contain understanding, acceptance and tolerance for diverse religions. It also entails a sense of self, curiosity and of awe and wonder along with learning values such as honesty and respect, right and wrong and accepting responsibility for the consequences of one's actions which ultimately leads to the development of responsibility, empathy and making moral decisions (Bradbury and Swailes, 2022; Mercer, 2018; Meggit, Bruce and Manning-Morton, 2016). As children grow older, they acquire a fuller knowledge and understanding of self, and become more able to self-regulate their actions and thinking (Early Years Coalition, 2021).

COGNITIVE DEVELOPMENT

Cognitive development includes changes in the way we think, understand and reason about the world (Charlesworth, 2016). It includes the accumulation of knowledge as well as the way we use that information and is related to the child's brain development which includes:

- the understanding of different concepts,
- processing information,
- memory,
- problem-solving and decision-making,
- analysing and being responsive about their thoughts,
- language and speech development.

(Bradbury and Swailes, 2022; Conkbayir, 2021; Mercer, 2018)

Each cognitive function activates a certain part of the brain, which helps a child understand, gain and use knowledge, and make meaning of the world (Early Years Coalition, 2021). Like other areas, children develop their cognitive abilities at different paces, which is determined by inborn preferences and previous experiences. Children learn best when they find something interesting and enjoyable to do, have a variety of experiences to choose from, are able to engage with others (adults and other children), experience a stimulating environment that encourages thinking and ideas and are accompanied by a supportive adult who is interested in what they are doing (DfE, 2021). Conkbayir and Pascal (2015) also talk about how learning needs to be planned based on a child's cognitive abilities. This is because each child's brain processes, responds, reasons, thinks and solves problems in a different way, and existing neuronal networks change in response to learning experiences.

REFLECTION

Consider the following when you are in placement:

- How does the learning environment and resources encourage young children with opportunities to explore and learn through all their senses?
- Are young children's learning experiences challenging their brains to respond actively and to assimilate information from a range of sources and ideas?
- How do the activities and resources stimulate young children whilst encouraging problem-solving?

ACTIVITY

Now we have reviewed holistic development and each of the domains consider the examples of holistic development and learning in the Birth to 5 Matters document (Early Years Coalition, 2021):

- Toddler eating his lunch: page 47
- Experimenting with water and construction: page 48

As you read through the above examples, consider the holistic development taking place.
Now reflect on an activity from your own practice

- What holistic development and learning occurred for the young children you supported?

CHILD DEVELOPMENT IN CONTEXT

This next section will explore child development in relation to the context in which children exist, drawing on the work of Bronfenbrenner (1989). Bronfenbrenner's belief was that a child is the product of their biology and their environment and questioned the usefulness of studies that theorised child development in unfamiliar situations (such as laboratory conditions). As graduate practitioners, the understanding of children's individual circumstances and learning journeys is key to effective pedagogy and practice in increasingly diverse communities and contexts. Bronfenbrenner is useful for considering individual development patterns and can be evidenced by detailed observations of children, activities to allow children's unique needs patterns and preferences to emerge as well as developing strategies to include parents and carers in these processes. Bronfenbrenner adapted his model many times over his life, the version we shall use is the bio-ecological model (Bronfenbrenner, 1989) which considers the chronosystem (see Figure 2.2).

Using the model to explore children's development ensures that we recognise that development does not happen in a vacuum; it is the direct consequence of interactions with a range of people and experiences in differing contexts. Disruption with interaction in one or more of the systems can negatively or positively impact what we think is 'normal development'. We must also consider cultural sensitivity, not just a child's faith and ethnicity but the culture within a child's unique living space. Families within the same faith and of the same ethnicity will differ in their approach to child rearing, their expectations of the child and long held beliefs and traditions around children, childhood and development (Bhatt, 2021). The implications for practice would require working alongside parents and sharing information about the child's homelife. Practitioners need to ensure that they regularly update their knowledge and understanding of child development and cultural difference. This can be evidenced to meet the ECGPCs in a range of ways such as the documentation the setting uses to gather information from parents and training certificates from continuing professional development (CPD) sessions and reflective accounts.

Ecological Systems Model
(Based on Bronfenbrenner, 1979)

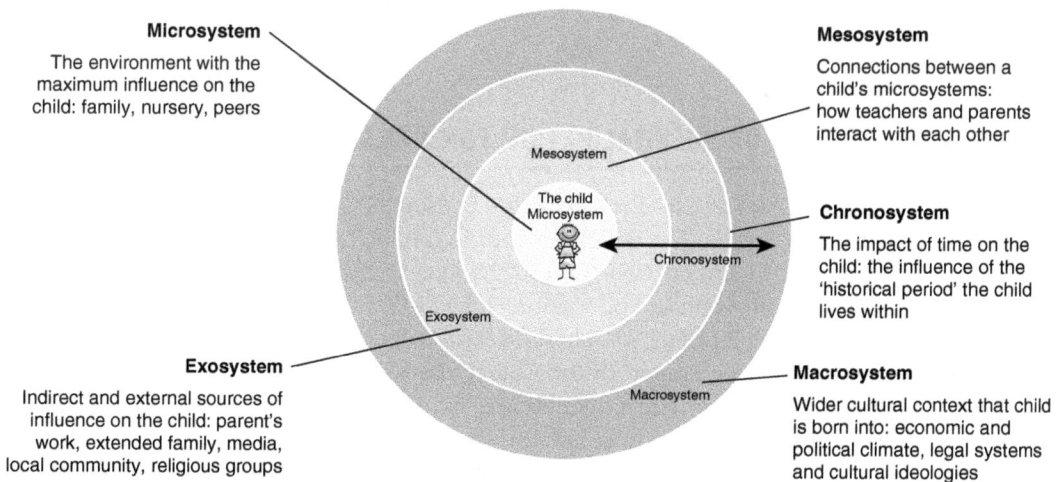

Microsystem
The environment with the maximum influence on the child: family, nursery, peers

Mesosystem
Connections between a child's microsystems: how teachers and parents interact with each other

Chronosystem
The impact of time on the child: the influence of the 'historical period' the child lives within

Exosystem
Indirect and external sources of influence on the child: parent's work, extended family, media, local community, religious groups

Macrosystem
Wider cultural context that child is born into: economic and political climate, legal systems and cultural ideologies

Figure 2.2 Bronfenbrenner's Bioecological System (1979)
Source: Taken from Grimmer, T in Bradbury, A., & Swailes, R. (2022). *Chapter 2: Bronfenbrenner. Early childhood theories today.*

BRONFENBRENNER IN PRACTICE

We can learn from Bronfenbrenner's ideas in two ways as we interrogate our practice and provision. Firstly, try putting ourselves in the centre of the model, and critically and honestly explore our own influences and possible bias and privilege. Doing so may help us to identify how these may inform any assumptions we have in relation to our understanding of children's development.

Secondly, Bronfenbrenner by his own admission reconsidered his ideas multiple times over his lifespan, stating that 're-assessing, revising, extending...regretting, renouncing' some of his earlier ideas (Bronfenbrenner, 1989, p. 187 in Vassa, 1989). This continuous state of revision of our practice and provision for individual children would ensure that we are meeting the needs of all, with regard for those who may need additional short-term or long-term support and intervention (GPC 6).

CHILDREN IN THE UNITED KINGDOM

The importance of Early Childhood Education and Care (ECEC) has informed government policy and been the subject of intervention programmes, such as curriculum guidance, workforce reform and accountability of provision (Moss, 2014). Reflecting on this in terms of the impact on children's development, according to Bronfenbrenner (1989), this mesosystem is the children's microsystem interacting with the exosystemic, which could result in some tensions. This political interest has manifested itself in England in documentation such as the Early Years Foundation Stage (DfE, 2021), Development Matters (Early Education, 2021) (there is also, Birth to 5 Matters, 2021), Ofsted involvement and interventions to 'professionalise' the workforce via higher academic qualifications (Moss, 2014). Northern Ireland, Wales and Scotland have developed ECEC curriculum and guidance frameworks. It is probably the surveillance documentation and the curriculum guidance which is more directly pertinent to our discussion as this directly relates to how we view 'normal' child development and our roles as early childhood educators.

THE POTENTIAL IMPACT OF HOSPITALISATION FOR CHILDREN

Bruce (1991) claimed that *children dance the ladder* of development, a metaphor to communicate the fragility around the development of a child. This has never been highlighted in research from sources including UNICEF (2021), Bhatt (2021), Department for Education (DfE) (2021a) and Early Intervention Foundation (EiF) (2021). The fragility around the factors that impact upon the development of children and especially can be illustrated by the restrictions imposed to limit the spread of the COVID pandemic.

The next section (see Figure 2.3) concentrates in how children's development can be affected by investigating children in hospital and the impact this can have on the child, and how we need to consider the professionals who work alongside to ensure the continued care of the child. Figure 2.3 emphasises the importance of how we care for children and the nurturing process of support they should receive from other professionals. Page (2017) highlighted this nurturing notion and evaluated that as professionals we should appreciate the

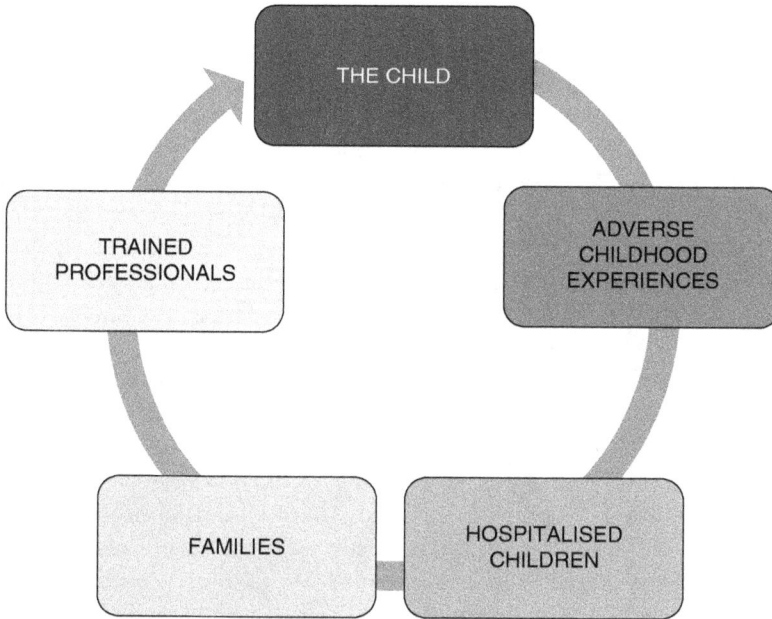

Figure 2.3 Holistic child: meeting their development and health needs

ethics of care and education for the children we support as children are central in this process and it is paramount that as early years practitioners, we recognise and understand this theory by working within those specialised boundaries (DfE, 2021) to facilitate children's development and progress.

HOSPITALISED CHILDREN

According to the Royal College of Paediatrics and Child Health (RCPCH) (2020), children are hospitalised for many reasons, some for long-term conditions such as cancer or epilepsy, some because they have been involved in road traffic accidents (RTA) and sometimes, a multitude of other factors which contribute to a visit or stay in hospital. As professionals we need to ask ourselves what does this mean for the child (and the family), and how does it affect them? The Healthcare Play Specialist Education Trust (2015) explained that children who are exposed to strange environments: people; tools; instruments, and most of all, separated from a primary carer can be challenging as it is detrimental in relation to the overall development of the child and can trigger the following feelings and behaviours:

- It can be intimidating and threatening.
- Children can feel helpless.
- It can exacerbate anxiety and increases stress levels.

(Tonkin, 2014)

These emotional behaviours can affect children in many ways. Musgrave (2017) has suggested ways that practitioners can support children who have a range of health conditions. The power of play can be used to alleviate stress and anxieties that may impact on children's behaviour either before (or after) a hospital procedure (as indicated above). Gulyurtlu et al. (2020) explain how this brings about many risks and challenges to a child's mental health as they are denied the safety of their normal routines. What does this really mean? A recent study from Hambrick et al. (2019) claims that early life stress (ELS) can impact on a child's development causing the trajectories to become skewed and trigger delays. Research from the 1950s to present day about hospitalised children has been instrumental in driving change to ensure children experience less stress, for example, the introduction of having a registered sick children nurses to care for them across a 24-hour period (Platt, 1959; Alsop-Sheilds and Mohay, 2001; Department of Health, 2003). Parents can visit their children at any time and stay with their child 24 hours a day. These initiatives are positive steps, but children in hospital need to have access to play that is organic and a natural part of childhood.

The UN Convention on the Rights of the Child (UNCRC) (2014) stated that *every child has the right to play* (Article 31). However, this is not always the case as some health authorities are unable to fund hospital play services, which leaves children feeling vulnerable; frightened and disempowered causing negative perceptions of hospitals and regression across behaviour patterns (Department of Health (DoH), 2003; Tonkin, 2014; Hospital Play Specialist Education Trust (HPSET), 2015). There is much research which has found that if children were informed about pre-procedures and more healthcare staff were trained to deliver this specialised preparation and play, children would accept what was happening to them and be able to stay in control and manage the process. Play is innovative as it enables children to work through fears, anxieties (Great Ormond Street, 2021) and much more; it helps children to self-regulate their emotions as it enables children to cope with intense emotions they may experience (Conkbayir, 2021) and behaviours (crucial in the care and education of children in hospital).

The question is why is this so important? Harvard University (2014) explains how the brain's architecture is affected by increased levels of anxiety and stress which in turn release hormones which impact on the ability to thrive and function, therefore, impacting on the overall development of the child.

CASE STUDY 2: NIGEL

Nigel, three years old, has been in a serious RTA and has a broken leg, arm, serious head injury and internal bleeding. Nigel is not from this area and his parents live in Worcester; Nigel will be in hospital for at least a month (if not longer). You are on duty when Nigel is taken up to the children's ward and while he has been sedated to ease the pain, in your role as an HPS you must consider your immediate thoughts about this child, their care and education while they are going to be a patient.

REFLECTION

Consider the following reflective questions in relation to the case study above:

- What emotions might this child exhibit?
- What should the HPS immediately consider about this child?
- How would you support Nigel and his family?
- What therapeutic play activities would you provide for Nigel and why?
- What are the theoretical links to your answer?
- What are the implications for your practice; how are you going to improve or change your practice when providing care and education for children who may be taken ill at a setting?
- How are you going to continue your professional development in relation to learning to understand how illness impacts on a child's holistic development?
- How do the ECSDN competencies connect with this situation and your role?

There are many factors to consider around working with children in hospital. As either the HPS in the hospital or practitioners in an ECEC setting, there is support and care you can offer children and families.

CHAPTER SUMMARY

At the beginning of this chapter, we identified aims that would explore and equip you to develop confidence, knowledge and understanding around factors which impacted on children's development, working with sick children and advancing your ECGPCs. We need to reflect on the importance of creating safe spaces and bear in mind the importance of routines because they provide consistency and security for children. Remain mindful about being observant around the cues a child or family present. You have the power to drive change and give children the best care and quality of education they so deserve!

FURTHER READING

Arnott, L. (2021) Holistic experiences: Celebrating the wonder of early childhood education. *International Journal of Early Years Education*. https://www.tandfonline.com/doi/pdf/10.1080/09669760.2021.2003949?needAccess=true

Musgrave, J. (2022) *Health and Wellbeing for Babies and Children. Contemporary Issues*. London: Routledge.

3

WORK DIRECTLY WITH YOUNG CHILDREN, FAMILIES AND COLLEAGUES TO PROMOTE HEALTH, WELL-BEING, SAFETY AND NURTURING CARE

Jackie Musgrave and *Aaron Bradbury*

CHAPTER ACKNOWLEDGEMENTS

With thanks to the following students and practitioners for their contributions:

Isobel Bailey, Paige Hall and Suzanne Fisher, Early Childhood Studies students at the University of Wolverhampton.

By the end of this chapter, you will be able to:

- Explore the factors which influence health and well-being for children and their families.
- Demonstrate the application of knowledge about health, well-being and safety to practice, including how these relate to your graduate practitioner competencies.
- Engage in the literature which supports the need for a robust critical knowledge of health and well-being.
- Demonstrate the ability to apply theory to early childhood practice while gathering evidence for your graduate practitioner competencies.
- Develop an ongoing dialogue of practice and theoretical concepts to gain graduate knowledge and continual understandings of health, well-being, safety and nurturing care.

KEY TERMS AND DEFINITIONS INCLUDED IN THIS CHAPTER

Term	Definition
Health	Health is a state of complete physical, mental and social well-being and not merely the absence of disease or infirmity (World Health Organization, 2018).
Physical health	The presence of a condition, which can be short term (acute) such as a cold or a stomach bug, or long term (chronic), such as asthma or diabetes.
Mental health	Mental health is defined as a state of well-being in which every individual realises their own potential, can cope with the normal stresses of life, can work productively and fruitfully and is able to make a contribution to their community (World Health Organization, 2018).
Mental health difficulty	Used to describe a variety of conditions children may experience, such as anxiety or depression which can be mild, moderate or severe. Other conditions include bipolar disorder, schizophrenia and eating disorders.
Health promotion	Health promotion is the process of enabling people to increase control over, and to improve, their health. It moves beyond a focus on individual behaviour towards a wide range of social and environmental interventions (World Health Organization, 2018).
Well-being	To do with the quality of people's lives, level of contentment and health.
Chronic health condition	A condition that is on going, lasts for longer than three months, is incurable and can affect daily life.
Acute health condition	A condition that is short-lived, usually of sudden onset and the symptoms of the condition usually disappear after a few days.
Complex medical needs	When a child requires extensive support with bodily functions, such as toileting, feeding or breathing to stay alive. Can be because of trauma or a genetic condition.

INTRODUCTION

This chapter explores how you will be able to demonstrate your competency in relation to promoting the health and well-being of babies and children in Early Childhood Education and Care (ECEC) settings. The content will help you to acquire the knowledge for Competency 3 and suggest ideas and knowledge that can be embedded into your practice.

COMPETENCY 3

3.1 Explain what factors influence health and well-being.

3.2 Demonstrate the application of knowledge about health, well-being and safety to practice, including:
- the importance of policies and legislation
- the identification of risks

(Continued)

(Continued)

- know how to identify and respond when a child is unwell or injured and may
- require urgent and non-urgent medical situations
- how to store and dispose of medicines
- practise good hygiene
- food preparation
- safe waste disposal
- how to use and maintain equipment and know how to access relevant training

3.3 Apply data protection legislation to practice.

3.4 Know and demonstrate how to complete a risk assessment and apply in practice.

3.5 Understand factors which influence nutritional health and integrate knowledge about current dietary guidance into practice, including early feeding and weaning.

3.6 Demonstrate the application of knowledge and understanding about the importance of respectful nurturing care routines including:
- personal care
- mealtime routines
- rest, sleep and 'quiet' time physical activity and mobility

3.7 Have relevant knowledge to support and manage children with on going health conditions.

3.8 Demonstrate how to promote health and educate children and families about health-related matters.

Our role as early childhood graduates gives many opportunities to promote children's health and well-being, and this is as a key part of keeping them safe, helping them to develop and supporting them to have positive outcomes into adulthood (Public Health England, 2021).

TERMS USED IN RELATION TO HEALTH

Health can be a difficult concept to define. Health can be a taken-for-granted concept; it is often only when we experience a period of feeling unwell or unhealthy that we start to appreciate good health.

There are many terms that are used in relation to health; some of the terms used in this chapter are defined in the table at the beginning of the chapter. The World Health Organization (WHO) definition of health in the table was first given in 1948, and it highlights that health relates to physical and mental health. However, physical and mental health can be interrelated. The presence of a physical condition that causes a range of symptoms such as pain, which can affect sleep patterns, appetite and so on, can cause depression and low self-esteem. It is important to note that negative experiences can adversely affect a child's mental and physical health, just as positive experiences are able to improve it. This can be seen in the research of the

Developing Child at Harvard University (2022) where they outline the importance of supporting holistic development for developing the child's brain.

The WHO definition states that health is not only to do with the absence of disease or infirmity, but this also implies that good health can be experienced even if a child has a health condition or a disability. This point links back to the importance of bearing in mind the uniqueness of each child.

Well-being is generally understood as the quality of people's lives. It is a dynamic state that is enhanced when people can fulfil their personal and social goals. It can be understood both in relation to being objective and measuring the impact of factors, such as household income, educational resources and outcomes and a person's health status. Subjective indicators such as happiness, the perceptions of quality of life and the impact on life satisfaction can also influence an individual's well-being. The concept of 'well-being' emerged from a more general discussion to de-medicalise health and encourage many governments to consider a wide range of factors which constituted poor health. The next section examines well-being in more detail.

DOMAINS AND MEASURES OF CHILDHOOD WELL-BEING

- Childhood well-being can be defined in many ways.
- A wide variety of domains and measures are used to assess levels of childhood well-being.
- The different domains and measures employed make it difficult to make meaningful comparisons of childhood well-being across different studies and different contexts.
- The different focus of well-being initiatives (for example, needs, poverty, quality of life, social exclusion and children's rights) has many implications for the type of policies and programmes that are supported.
- There is a growing consensus that childhood well-being is multi-dimensional, should include dimensions of physical, emotional and social well-being; should focus on the immediate lives of children but also consider their future lives; and should incorporate objective and subjective measures.

(Statham and Chase, 2010)

The following case study by Isobel Paige sets the scene for the content of this chapter.

CASE STUDY 1: WHY IS COMPETENCY 3 IMPORTANT? THE STUDENT'S VIEW

ISOBAL PAIGE

Placement, university and the Early Childhood Graduate Practitioner Competencies (ECGPC) have allowed me to develop my knowledge of personal care as I have been able to observe practice and actively take part in promoting this as part of the daily routine. Furthermore, my understanding from the Early Years Foundation Stage (EYFS) Statutory Framework (DfE, 2021) Early Learning Goals 'Managing Self' outlines the importance of the child managing 'their own basic hygiene and personal needs, including dressing

(Continued)

(Continued)

and going to the toilet...' (p. 11). Personal care is covered within Competency 3 which states 'Work directly with young children, families, and colleagues to promote health, well-being, safety and nurturing care' (Early Childhood Studies Degree Network, 2020, p. 15). Competency 3 itself allows a broad span of areas that as practitioners we should encourage such as oral hygiene, food preparation, hand washing and rest and sleep routines. It has enabled me to develop a new way of thinking and understanding of what personal care really means for each unique child as I am learning about supporting children's needs at different ages and stages. A key way in which I developed the skills to understand this was by exploring my setting and finding the different ways that they may promote personal care. This was effective as I was able to discover new ways of understanding what personal care meant to my setting and how they encouraged this.

COMMENTARY ON CASE STUDY 1

Isobel's words illustrate how she became familiar with the health-related aims and principles of the EYFS and the ECGPCs. Through her placement experience, she was able to observe the practical implementation of the routines that are the foundations of good health, such as sleep and the provision of food. She also highlights how practitioners can promote good health and prevent infections by supporting children with self-care routines, such as hand washing.

Isobel draws our attention to the role of nurturing in relation to young children. Nurturing engages children in the human community in ways that support them to define who they are, what they can become and why they are important to other people.

THE UNIQUE CHILD

Isobel refers to the uniqueness of each child and considering the individuality of each child in the context of health is of critical importance. It is important to consider how you can address the health needs of children who have a physical health condition or a disability. Children with complex medical are likely to require further consideration.

Knowing the babies and children in your care will help you to recognise when they are unwell. Supporting children's health can be challenging, partly because babies and children's ability to let us know how they feel depends on their age, level of development and the context of their lives. Young children may not have the vocabulary to describe how they are feeling. If children are asked where their tummy aches, they may point to their head.

We can support children's health by knowing what to do about the following:

- Understanding our role in supporting children in maintaining good levels of health.
- How to engage with health promotion for both the child and the family.
- Knowing what to when a child is feeling or becomes unwell.

Children with on going health conditions, such as diabetes or asthma, will benefit from your knowledge of how to minimise the impact of the symptoms of their health condition. Ongoing, or chronic, health conditions affect as many as 27% of children (Wijlaars, Gilbert and Hardelid, 2016); therefore, understanding how such conditions affect children's health is an important area of practice to consider. For example, cold weather and physical exercise can be a trigger for asthma symptoms. However, the simple step of encouraging a child who has asthma to wear a scarf over their mouths so that the air they breathe in is warmed can prevent asthma symptoms from being provoked. Therefore, knowing how to prevent symptoms from being triggered can mean that the child will not be excluded from taking part in outdoor physical activity because of a health condition.

REFLECTION

Consider the children in your setting, how may their unique needs require you to adapt routines and care to ensure that you are supporting their health effectively?

FACTORS THAT INFLUENCE CHILDREN'S HEALTH AND WELL-BEING

There are numerous factors that influence children's health; examples of some of these factors are summarised in Figure 3.1.

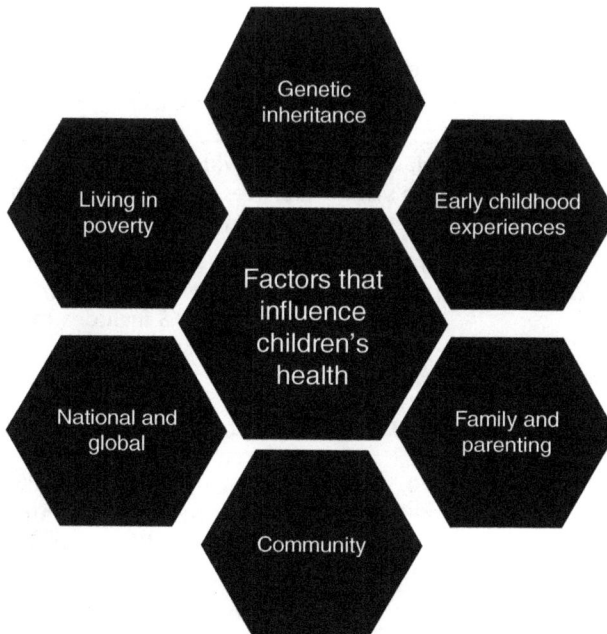

Figure 3.1 The factors that influence health and well-being

Children's health can be influenced by factors before conception takes place, the importance of pre-conceptual care can be under-regarded. Genetic conditions can be passed on from parents to the baby. The mother's health and the quality of pre-natal care can influence babies' and children's health.

Children's early experiences can impact on their physical and mental health. Children thrive when they can benefit from positive relationships. This can be seen in the words of Bronfenbrenner (1994): '....to develop normally, a child requires progressively more complex joint activity with one or more adults who have an irrational emotional relationship with the child. Somebody's got to be crazy about that kid. That's number one. First, last, and always' (Bradbury, 2022, p. 7).

For many children, the people who are 'crazy about that kid' are the parents; however, not all children are born into a loving family. Children who experience adverse childhood experiences such as neglect and abuse are likely to have poorer health outcomes.

The community that a child lives in can impact positively or negatively on children's health. Communities that have safe, well-maintained play areas and provide access to children's services are likely to have children who are healthier than children who live in poorer areas.

The country that a child lives in influences children's health, for example, many countries across the world provide free immunisations. Immunisations help to reduce the possibility of children developing infectious diseases that can be fatal or can leave children with a legacy of disability.

The most significant factor that negatively impacts on children's health is living in poverty and poverty exists in all countries of the world.

POLICY AND LEGISLATION RELATING TO CHILDREN'S HEALTH

Table 3.1 summarises some policies and guidance aimed at improving children's health.

Table 3.1 Policy and legislation related to children's health

Legislation	Aim
Best Start in Life (Public Health England, 2021) Healthy child programme 0 to 19: health visitor and school nurse commissioning	To provide universal and targeted public health services provided by health visiting and school nursing teams
Statutory guidance: EYFS statutory framework (Department for Education, 2021a)	Sets standards for the learning, development and care of your child from birth to five years old. The EYFS includes more than 30 health related aims
Policy/Guidance/Reports	**Aim**
Keeping children safe in education (2022)	Safeguarding and promoting the welfare of children is defined for the purposes of this guidance as: protecting children from maltreatment; preventing impairment of children's health or development
Children's Alliance working group reports	Four reports aimed at changing policy at senior government level to promote the health and well-being of children in their early years

Table 3.1   Policy and legislation related to children's health   (Continued)

Legislation	Aim
National Institute for Health and Care Excellence (NICE)	Publishes guidance advice and quality standards for children and young people's health related issues – 187 sets of guidance available
All direct links to the above documents are available at the end of this chapter.	

APPLYING KNOWLEDGE ABOUT HEALTH, WELL-BEING AND SAFETY TO PRACTICE

This section summarises some of the knowledge that you will need to make links to and develop your practice. The content will explore how policy and legislation help to inform practice. A broad range of issues relating to how you keep children healthy are examined. It is worth bearing in mind that in England, the EYFS has more than 30 aims and principles that if implemented effectively in practice will help to promote and support the health of all children (Musgrave, 2021).

Policies around health, well-being and safety within settings help to develop good practice; gain better health outcomes; provide consistency; and enhance knowledge and understanding.

CARE ROUTINES AND HEALTH

Consistent routines that meet the physical needs of children are important for their health and well-being and help to build the foundations of good health both in childhood and across the lifespan.

Supporting children's physical care practices includes the following routines shown in Figure 3.2:

The routines illustrated above all make a contribution to children's good health. The provision of good nutrition and hydration in education settings carries significant responsibilities; the following section explores this aspect of health in more depth.

NUTRITION

Providing babies and children with good nutrition and promoting healthy eating habits are part of the foundation of good health. Practitioners play a key role in this aspect of health.

NUTRITION FOR BABIES

Many settings provide care for babies who are very young, and it is important to consider how their nutritional needs can be met. Nutrition for babies in the first six months is provided by milk, either formula or human milk, which can be given by bottle or breast. Whichever mode of delivery, practitioners have an important role to support early nutrition.

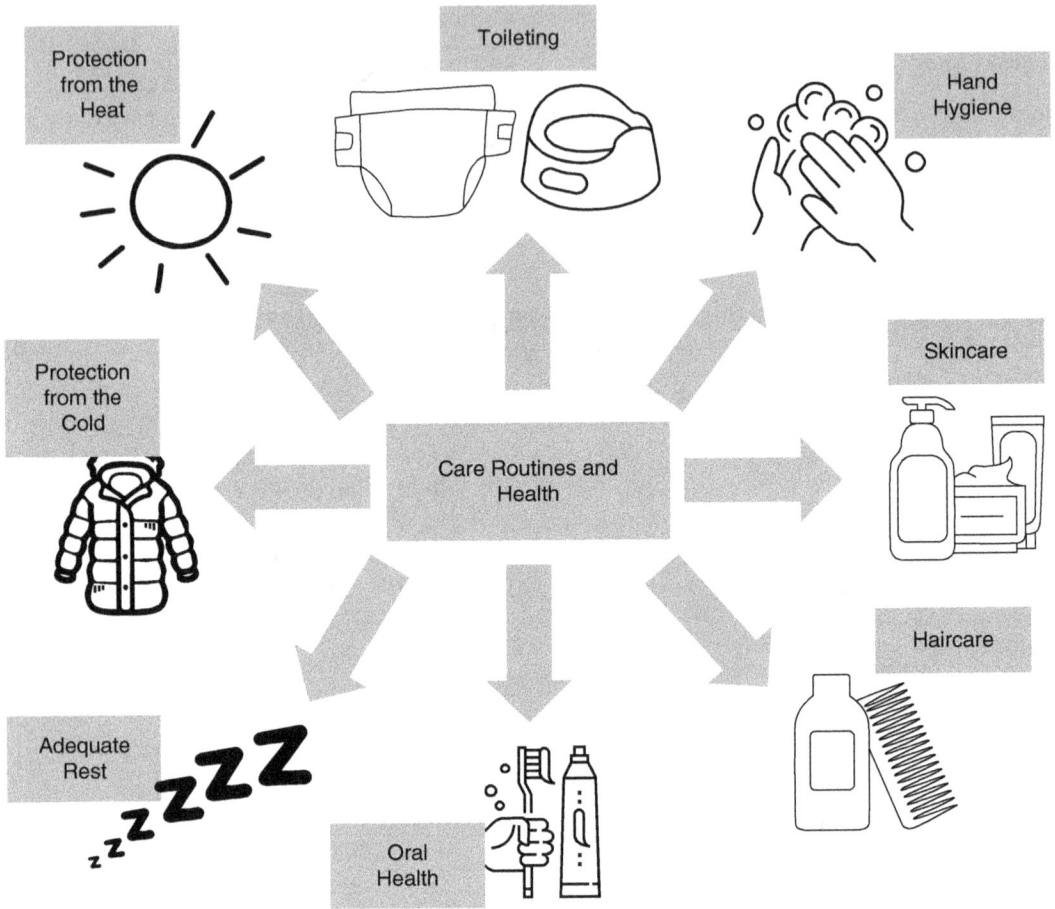

Figure 3.2 Care routines that support children's health

WEANING OR COMPLEMENTARY FEEDING

Moving from a milk-based diet to solid foods is described as weaning, or complementary feeding. Guidance about when and how to introduce babies to solid foods varies around the world. In England, as in many high-income countries, it is advised that complementary feeding is introduced when babies are six months old. There is a trend to offer babies the opportunity to self-wean, meaning that they are offered a selection of food and they can choose what they eat.

NUTRITION FOR YOUNG CHILDREN

Children may not distinguish between food that they like and foods that are healthy. Children frequently display 'neophobia', a fear of new foods, but it is important to persevere with introducing a range of new foods to their diet.

Nutrition matters for young children so please take on board the following points shown in Figure 3.3:

Children's appetites may vary, not only from day to day, but also from one meal to the next.	Puddings should be nutritious and based on milk and/or fruit (fresh, stewed or tinned)
Children should be encouraged to drink adequate amounts of fluids.	Don't add salt as babies' kidneys are not fully developed.
Young children are very active and have high energy (calorie) and nutrient needs in proportion to their small body size.	Foods and drinks containing sugar should only be given occasionally and should be limited to mealtimes.
A frequent intake of sugar and sugary foods and drinks between meals causes tooth decay. Snacks and drinks taken between meals should be sugar-free.	Whole-nuts are not advised under the age of five years because of the risk of choking. It is recommended that peanuts and products containing them are not provided. This is to protect children who may be at risk of nut allergies.

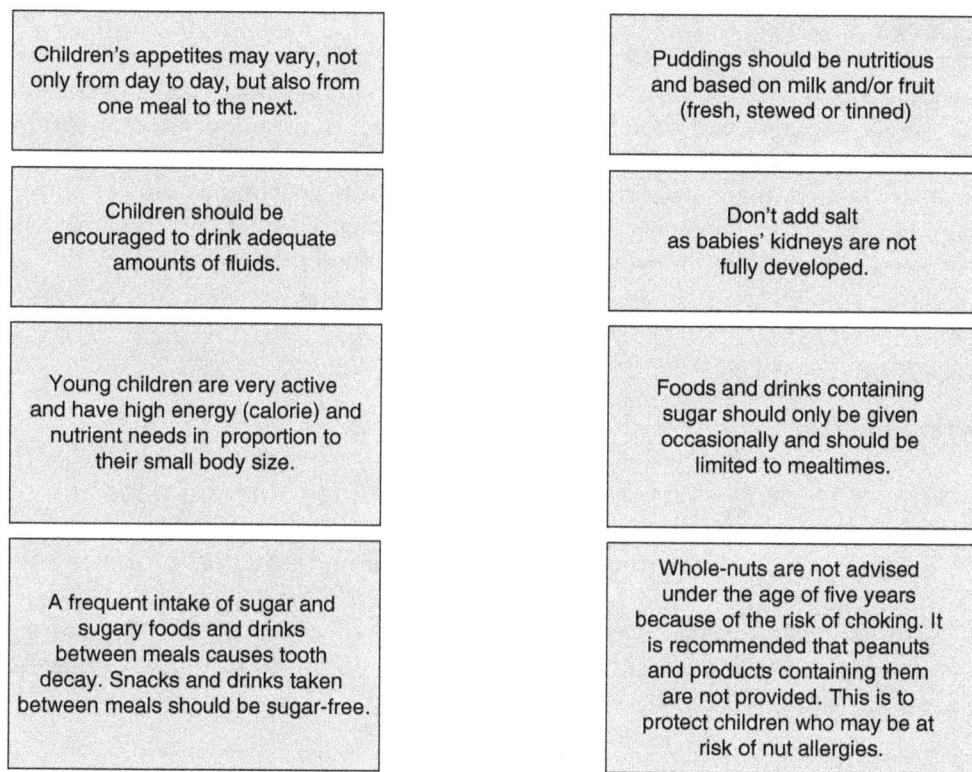

Figure 3.3   Children's nutrition: key points to consider

In the following case study, Paige Hall explains how she linked her practice to Competency 3.

CASE STUDY 2: PREPARING FOOD

When preparing food, it was vital to adhere to previous food hygiene training and guidance in the EYFS section 3.49, where it states that there must be suitable facilities for the hygienic preparation of food, and those involved in preparing and handling food must receive food hygiene training (Department for Education, 2021). To ensure this was actioned, I and another educator first washed our hands, and prepped the area and chopping boards. Then, as per Public Health England's (2017) recommendations, we thoroughly washed the fruits, removed any pips and chopped them into the appropriate sizes. This experience gave me the affordances to learn the importance of Competency 3 in practice and the effects it can have on young children. In my current placement in Year 1, if I were to do something similar, I may demonstrate to them how and where to safely prepare foods and why.

CASE STUDY 2 COMMENTARY

In this case study, Paige explains how she is practising safe preparation of food for children; she emphasises the importance of good hygiene in order to reduce the risk of infection that may be passed on through unsafe food, and which in turn could cause ill health. Her comments demonstrate her understanding of the link between statutory guidance as laid out in the EYFS (DfE, 2021), with the requirements of Competency 3.5. Interestingly, Paige also acknowledges that she has a responsibility to teach children about safe food preparation.

REFLECTION

During mealtimes do you consider the following?

- Ways to provide nourishing food and hydration that are good for children's health.
- Routines that help to develop a sense of community and promote social interactions.
- Safety considerations, such as prevention of choking, being aware of allergies, and dietary restrictions. Knowing what to do in an emergency, such as anaphylaxis.

MANAGING CHILDREN WITH DIETARY NEEDS AND RESTRICTIONS

It is also important to remember that many children may need additional support in the provision of nutrition. For example, children may have complex medical needs which means they need to be tube fed, or they may have intolerance or an allergy to foods.

In the following case study, Isobel writes about how being on placement helped her to learn about nutrition and children's health. In the first part, she explores her role in relation to healthy eating for all children. In the second part, she looks at the nutritional need of children who have an intolerance or allergy to foods.

CASE STUDY 3: PAIGE HALL

When starting placement, I had a limited understanding of the importance of food preparation and safe eating routines (allergies, special diets, intolerances). However, through the combination of module content and the ECGPC, I have been able to implement activities and adapt my placement practice. Completing a general health needs analysis (HNA) within my setting for three-to five-year-olds led me to understand children's health needs and the risks they pose. Allen (2011) noted the first five years of a child's life are

(Continued)

(Continued)

the most important when determining their future outcomes. In addition to the HNA, this underlines the value of instilling healthy eating habits in children early, to prevent any potential detrimental ramifications later in life, and communicating such lessons to parents (Bristow et al., 2011).

While working to meet Competency 3, I was able to work directly with young children and families and have professional discussions with educators. I became informed about children's special diets because of religious or health reasons. My understanding of individual educational health care (EHC) Plans, which include any special dietary needs such as allergies, was influenced by the material I was taught in modules. My placement, however, afforded me the chance to put what I had learned about the implications and significance of safe eating routines into practice, and I regularly observed how the educator's prepared food for snack time, food tastings and celebrations such as Diwali. If parents chose, they could withdraw their child from the activity.

Fruits that were to be used to produce fruit kebabs were carefully chosen, and EHC plans were reviewed for current allergies and intolerances. For instance, one child had a severe allergy to the taste, touch and smell of oranges; another had a severe intolerance to all red foods, so red apples had to be replaced with green ones. These allergies were noted in the risk assessment, along with procedures, such as the need for first aid, in case of a choking hazard (Public Health England, 2017). It also included possible medications that may be needs, such as an epi-pen, in the event of a child having an anaphylactic reaction.

CASE STUDY 3 COMMENTARY

Paige describes how planned an activity that was designed to help the children in her setting to identify healthy food choices; let's take a deeper look at some of the learning from the case study and reflect on the learning:

- **The importance of policies in safe food preparation**
  - Providing healthy eating for children is a statutory requirement of the EYFS (2021).
  - An education healthcare plan helps to summarise how a child's dietary needs should be met, thus reducing risk of harm to the child.
  - Paige did a health needs analysis to help her identify the potential risks that may be posed to the children because of their engagement with the activity. She includes the need to ensure that there is access to an epi-pen for a child with anaphylaxis.

- **Children who require additional consideration with their nutritional needs**
  - o What is healthy for one child is not necessarily a healthy choice for all children. Some children may have severe allergies, anaphylaxis, to foods which can be life-threatening.
  - o Intolerance to foods – for example, a child who has been diagnosed with coeliac disease is intolerant to gluten (which is present in wheat flour, rye and barley). This is not necessarily a fatal consequence, but inadvertently consuming gluten can cause discomfort and damage to the intestine.
  - o Parental choice and cultural considerations such as food for celebrations need to be thought about.

REFLECTION

Consider your experience of managing children's dietary needs in your practice

- Do you have anything further to add to the points made above?
- Can you add any other considerations? For example, what would you need to consider for a child with a physical disability or one that required tube feeding?

In the following case study, Suzanne explores how she developed her knowledge about oral health in order to meet Competence 3.

CASE STUDY 4: SUZANNE FISHER

Public Health England (2017) stated that tooth decay is a serious health issue that is largely preventable. In their 2015 survey, they found 25% of children in England had experienced tooth decay, with an average of 3–4 teeth being affected. 41% of these children can be accounted for due to deprivation. Poor oral health can have several implications for children including pain, tooth extraction, lost hours of education, infections, difficulties eating and sleeping, as well as an impact on socialising. Implications for the family can include stress and loss of earnings, for a family already struggling financially and with the current cost of living crisis this could push more families into poverty or even deeper poverty.

Through my engagement with colleagues at placement, I learnt that dental care is now part of the Early Years Foundation Stage (DfE, 2021) as it is an important factor in obtaining school readiness and a good state of overall health. I was lucky enough to be involved in a visit from the dentist while at

(Continued)

(Continued)

placement recently, the children were excited about the visit and the level of engagement from 50+ 4–5-year-olds was incredible. In the week leading up to the visit the parents were notified by email about the importance of good oral hygiene and foods they should avoid giving their children.

The dentist started the discussion with brightly decorated show cards of different foods, and she allowed the children to tell her whether they were 'good' or 'bad' foods. The children were all very knowledgeable about what categories the foods fell into, which reiterated to me, the importance of oral health in the curriculum. By being involved in this activity, it has highlighted the importance of oral health as previously I would not have thought lack of oral health could have an impact on the development of children or an impact on their school readiness status. This activity has also helped me to write a health needs analysis for one of my level 5 modules. As a developing professional, I now understand that I need to always promote good oral hygiene and further activities I can develop include bingo games with healthy foods, books available to support good oral hygiene.

CASE STUDY 4 COMMENTARY

Suzanne articulates clearly in this case study how her engagement with the activities aimed at improving good oral health for the children has helped her to improve her knowledge about this issue. Her experience highlights the important role that education settings play in promoting health. Inviting a dentist to visit the children to increase their knowledge is an example of good practice.

ACTIVITY

Think of an activity you could provide in your setting regarding the case study above.

Here are some of the things you could think about

- Health Promotion – Display boards and leaflets.
- Activities around oral hygiene – Each child has a toothbrush and toothpaste for brushing after meals.
- Parent/carer play sessions with a focus on oral hygiene.

HEALTH PROMOTION AND THE ROLE OF ECEC PRACTITIONERS

Promoting good health needs to start from birth because our habits are formed very early in life. And practitioners working in ECEC settings are ideally placed to make a valuable contribution to health promotion as Musgrave and Payler (2021) found out in their research with practitioners in an area of high deprivation. Key to successful health promotion for babies and young children is a need to work in partnership with parents. The practitioners also used opportunities such as the Nursery open evening for parents to display information aimed at educating parents about healthy eating. Figure 3.4 shows the display that was made to illustrate to parents the amount of sugar content in foods that were regularly provided in children's lunch boxes (Musgrave, 2019). Importantly, the practitioners provided examples of low-cost and healthier options for parents to consider including in their children's lunches (Figure 3.4).

Figure 3.4   Health education display about sugar content in lunch box content

ACTIVITY

Review and write down some notes in response to the following questions. Try to offer an honest and critical stance as this will support you and your professional development within this area.

Take some time to pause and reflect. Consider the following questions to support your graduate practice in meeting the graduate practitioner competencies (GPCs):

*   How are you going to ensure your knowledge of government legislative and statutory requirements is current?
*   How will you identify how these are articulated into setting policy?

What further action may you need to take in meeting the above questions? How will you demonstrate critical links between your knowledge and professional practice for your GPC evidence?

CHAPTER SUMMARY

This chapter has highlighted the contribution you can make to promote the health of babies and young children. The case studies give practical ideas of how to work with children and parents to educate them about health. The content highlights how many health promoting activities are embedded in everyday routines, such as the provision of nutrition and care routines. You are encouraged to consider terms such as 'healthy eating' and consider that what is healthy for one child may be unhealthy, and in fact may be life threatening for a child who has anaphylaxis. You are encouraged to become familiar with policy and legislation that is aimed at keeping children healthy and safe, as well as committing to learning more about how you can promote children's health. How children's physical and mental health is addressed in the earliest months and years of life has impact across the lifespan. We all have a responsibility to ensure that we are competent in maximising their potential to be healthy.

FURTHER READING

Cazaly, H. (2022) *Young Children's Health and Wellbeing from Birth to 11*. London: Learning Matters.

Musgrave, J. (2022) *Health and Wellbeing for Babies and Children: Contemporary Issues*. Abingdon: Routledge.

4

OBSERVE, LISTEN AND PLAN FOR YOUNG CHILDREN TO SUPPORT THEIR WELL-BEING, EARLY LEARNING, PROGRESSION AND TRANSITIONS

Dawn Jones and *Selena Hall*

CHAPTER ACKNOWLEDGEMENTS

With thanks to the following students and practitioners for their contributions:

Student contributions Freshta Majid, Catherine Pass, Gemma Simpson, Kizzy Scott, Bethaney Whitehouse, Karielle Brown and Tara Andrew

By the end of this chapter, you will be able to:

- Develop the skills required to observe children's well-being, early learning, progression and transitions in early childhood.
- Demonstrate your understanding of the purpose of observations to support planning for children's next steps, while acknowledging the ways to promote and support the individual needs of children.
- Engage in ways to support and promote the holistic learning and well-being of children as you progress and develop through practice-based learning.
- Demonstrate your emerging ability to note key aspects and themes acknowledged through undertaking observations.
- Make cohesive links between theories and concepts in relation to your early childhood graduate practitioner competencies.

KEY TERMS AND DEFINITIONS INCLUDED IN THIS CHAPTER

Observing children	To step and back and note the in-the-moment interactions between the child, environment and resources.
Transition	Changes in routine and their daily lives that impact and influence their childhood.
Planning	Preparing, reflecting and reviewing the child's next steps based upon the needs, interests and holistic development gained from observing children.
Supporting learning	Making use of underpinning knowledge, theory and practice to offer child centred practice that can be adult led.
Supporting well-being	Advocating for the child and family through partnership working. celebrating the uniqueness of children and their families.

INTRODUCTION

This chapter discusses and examines Competency 4 in relation to the importance of observations in supporting the unique child. It asks you to consider and recognise the wide range of experiences that they (children) bring with them; while also acknowledging the rich learning opportunities that this affords us as professional early childhood practitioners. Observations enable us to assess young children's learning, but to do so effectively practitioners need to firstly understand what they are seeing and watching. To understand how to unpick and use this information to support the young child's individual holistic development, Competency 4 should be considered alongside your developing understanding, enabling you to examine your practice through application of practical experiences.

COMPETENCY 4: OBSERVE, LISTEN AND PLAN FOR YOUNG CHILDREN TO SUPPORT THEIR WELL-BEING, EARLY LEARNING, PROGRESSION AND TRANSITIONS

4.1 Know and understand the relevant early childhood curriculum frameworks and apply them in practice.

4.2 Apply a range of observation and research skills to co-construct young children's development, play and learning, encouraging independence and next steps.

4.3 Evidence the application of different theoretical perspectives when planning for young children's personal, social and emotional development.

4.4 Apply theoretical understanding to the range of transitions young children experience and how these can be effectively supported in practice.

(Continued)

(Continued)

4.5 Evidence knowledge of the importance of parents and/or caregivers and the home learning environment in infants and young children's development and learning.

4.6 Demonstrate knowledge and skill in listening to and communicating verbally and non-verbally with children and how to encourage their communication skills, including situations where:

English is an additional language.
A child has special educational needs and/or disabilities.

4.7 Identify and apply pedagogical knowledge of how to develop enabling environments indoors and outdoors.

4.8 Explain and demonstrate understanding of the balance between child-led and adult-led activities.

4.9 Using real world contexts apply to practice theoretical understanding of:

Language development
Literacy development (including early reading and writing)
Mathematical concepts

4.10 Evidence contemporary knowledge and skills in the use of technology and the role and appropriate use of digital literacies in young children's learning.

4.11 Enable young children to understand the wider world.

The process of understanding children through observing and listening as a developing professional will be explored throughout this chapter. The foundations of the discussions shall be based upon Early Childhood Studies undergraduate students from the University of Wolverhampton. Three case studies written by students will share their placement experiences and how these experiences have assisted them to build upon and develop their early childhood graduate practitioner competency (ECGPC) evidence. Case Study 1 discusses the experiences of a level 4 student at the start of their observation journey, where they engage with key learning surrounding the use and purpose of observations in a school setting in the West Midlands. These real-life experiences from practice will provide a meaningful context upon which to discuss and demonstrate how Competency 4 can be applied and thus understood in practice. The second case study draws upon a level 4 student's experience of acknowledging and supporting the individual needs of children. These reflections were completed towards the end of level 4 study during the student's time in a Nursery setting within the West Midlands. Through acknowledging the diversity of children, you will then be able to draw upon and make sense of Competency 4. The final case study, completed in a Nursery setting in the West Midlands by a level 6 student, examines opportunities to promote holistic development based upon child-centred practice. These shared placement experiences from a student's perspective will be relatable and support you in identifying connections between theoretical perspectives and academic study. Furthermore, these case study extracts will support you to engage with and apply strategies. These promote an understanding of what high standards of care to support well-being, early learning, progression and transitions look like within a professional body. While being underpinned by reference to the Birth to 5 Matters theme of 'the unique child' in the 'everchanging context' (The Early Years Coalition, 2021) this chapter will provide reflective questions for you to reflect and draw upon as a developing professional. We will begin this chapter with three case studies demonstrating Competency 4 in practice

The first extract below offers an insight upon a student's initial experiences of engaging with and implementing the observation cycle. The following contextual placement experience as well as real-life events are fundamental within this chapter. Providing relatable experience of how graduate competencies, specifically Competency 4 can be usefully applied to everyday practice with young children.

THE OBSERVATION CYCLE

CASE STUDY 1: CATHERINE PASS

Before starting work placement my understanding of observations was limited. From my experiences in my first year of study, observations are the prime way to understand the unique and wonderful personalities each child has and in turn how we, as developing professionals, can meet these differing needs that are held. The term 'observations' initially seemed simple leading me to conclude that its impact and purpose could be overlooked. Upon reflection, observing in the context of education is different; it is critical to the development of children and, therefore, our professional practice. In particular, I found the Birth to 5 Matters (The Early Years Coalition, 2021) very helpful. This document outlines how observations are a great way to get to grips with how children learn and interact. Something I found that emphasised the motivation of observation is its explanation of how different children act when they feel a sense of freedom. This sums up the importance of observations perfectly as they are the truest, most genuine accounts we can get of children as they develop. With regards to undertaking observations in placement I developed a sense of observing the surroundings and identifying a few elements of importance. A key way I have developed my observational skills is by having guidelines, such as what I was hoping to achieve by observing the children. This meant my observations led to an end goal or a purpose. This was presented through the cultivation of my ECGPC portfolio. For

(Continued)

(Continued)

example, Competency 4.4 talks about how through the use of observations we can support children's well-being when experiencing transitions. Here, I have been given a target that allows me to focus upon a purpose. A child at my first placement was struggling with separation anxiety when arriving at school. This child would often express a need to be with their parent/guardian. During this transition the child became stressed, and this led to them withdrawing from interacting with other children. The setting used various strategies to ensure this child felt more comfortable and secure, for example, having a familiar and friendly face to greet them every morning. This measure proved to be effective and wouldn't have been achieved without myself as the student and the other practitioners using observations. When developing my observational skills, I began to further understand the significance and acknowledge the need to develop and practice my use of observations, as well as target setting which was essential before and after undertaking observations so that they had the most impact.

COMMENTARY ON CASE STUDY 1

Catherine discusses the importance of frameworks and how they can offer ideas and support for practitioners both at the start of their professional journey but also as a useful guide for those with perhaps more experience, therefore, responding to **4.1 Know and understand the relevant early childhood curriculum frameworks and apply them in practice**. The importance of how Catherine sees her role as one of observing from afar, capturing the children's joy and engagement and the role that the environment plays within this are all interesting points to examine. Consider the importance of capturing what we refer to as 'the all' so what is the child playing with or indeed alongside, and what influence does this have upon the play sequence? What I am suggesting is the resource or materials prompts a response, so are essential (Pacini-Ketchabaw, Kind and Kocher, 2017). Where are they situated, does the natural world have any input within the play, so is it windy, are their shadows, rain and so on. Take time to consider 'the all' as this can provide as Catherine suggests a wealth of valuable information upon which planning to meet the child's holistic needs can be utilised. Consider how this relates to and supports **4.2 Apply a range of observation and research skills to co-construct young children's development, play and learning, encouraging independence and next steps**. The importance of the environment has long been acknowledged as an important element as noted by White (2014), Joyce (2012) and Boyd, Hirst and Siraj-Blatchford (2018). Catherine highlights that the role of the environment is significant and, therefore, should be reflected upon. Again, consider how this draws upon and supports **4.11 *Enable young children to understand the wider world***.

REFLECTION

Catherine refers to ECGPC 4.4 Apply theoretical understanding to the range of transitions young children experience and how these can be effectively supported in practice.

- In what ways would the key person make use of the observations to support children's well-being as they experience transitions?
- Consider how you could examine attachment theory in relation to transitions experienced in early childhood?
- Refer to the Birth to 5 Matters or The Early Years Foundation Stage (Department for Education 2021) Guidance. What guidance do these documents offer surrounding the use of observations for practitioners?

Birth to 5 Matters (The early years Coalition, 2021) details that in practice we should offer a responsive pedagogy that guides us to understand, recognise and know what children can do. This document offers contemporary suggestions for developing child centred practice. As a student the Birth to 5 Matters guidance enables you to situate the graduate competencies within your practice thus bringing together your academic knowledge and practice-based experiences. A key aspect of your role is to *'Know and understand the relevant Early Childhood curriculum frameworks and apply them in practice' (Competency 4.1).* Therefore, enabling you to demonstrate how the graduate competencies contribute and extend your knowledge as a developing professional.

INDIVIDUAL CHILDREN'S INTERESTS AND CULTURAL IDENTITIES

Case Study 2 focuses upon the importance of observations as a tool to grasp how the recognition of individual children's interests and cultural identity can promote strategies that specifically meet the unique needs of the child. An important aspect of this extract is the collaboration between the student and the professional partner and the shared learning experience that takes place.

CASE STUDY 2: FRESHTA MAJID

My placement counts as one of my positive milestones. It was challenging at first, however it vastly improved my knowledge of early childhood development as well as the ECGPCs which were initially unfamiliar. Child-led play was interesting to me because, in my country, children do not attend settings until they are five years old, apart from day-care,

(Continued)

(Continued)

where the perspective of children learning through play differs. The placement gave me the opportunity to interact while enabling me to examine children's learning and development making connections to the theorists learnt during my module study. My curiosity to understand children's development allowed me to learn how to observe within an early childhood setting, which was a new skill for me. We can observe children at play in order to gain a better understanding of their abilities, interests and needs. 'We can discover more about a person in an hour of play than in a year of conversation' (Plato in Smidt, 2010, p. 1). The concept of observing children extends beyond caring for them, monitoring their health and teaching them. According to Dyer and Taylor (2012), practitioners must understand how children learn and develop, how to meet a child's particular development needs and how observation and evaluation can guide the planning and implementation to facilitate children's learning and development. During this placement, I had a chance to work with children who speak English as an Additional Language (EAL) or have special educational needs (SEN). I noticed how children's actions, gestures and interests differ as well as the ways distraction strategies were used by the practitioners in my setting to engage children. The professional partner supporting me in placement advised me and guided me to develop these and other communication methods and techniques. The EYFS (DFE, 2021) highlights the importance of observation and following the interests of the child. I have reflected on my learning this year and I believe that a good practitioner effectively observes children. As I progress to the next level of study and within my practice, I will continue to practise observing children to broaden my knowledge and strengthen my understanding.

COMMENTARY ON CASE STUDY 2

Freshta discusses the importance of working alongside the professional partner within her placement setting, asking questions and discussing the various happenings of the day, thus helping to support the embedding of the graduate competencies within your practice. Being able to reflect upon those experiences and building confidence further develops your knowledge and is an extremely important aspect of your professional practice. It also provides rich evidence for your ECGPC portfolios. Nolan and Molla (2018) support Freshta as they agree that learning takes place when situated in active practice. Freshta was able to observe not only the children but also how the practitioners worked alongside the children to support them. She notes distraction strategies, and alternative modes of communication, therefore developing a whole set of new skills for her professional toolbox. The individual needs of the child are discussed, and Freshta highlights the importance of this in relation to then meeting and extending the child's learning. This case study also shows how Freshta is beginning to make links between theory and practice, how they complement and support each other. Perhaps you can reflect upon your experiences within placement and identify theory in action as Freshta has.

REFLECTION

Freshta has begun to identify and make links to Competency 4.6: Demonstrate knowledge and skill in listening to and communicating verbally and non-verbally with children and how to encourage their communication skills, including situations where:

a. English is an Additional Language.
b. A child has special educational needs and/or disabilities.
   - How could this rich and detailed information about the children be used to effectively support early learning and progression?
   - Reflect upon the importance of working with parents as partners in the observation, assessment and planning cycle.
   - How might observations feed into inter-agency working when planning for the holistic development needs of the child?

OBSERVING THE CHILD AT DIFFERENT INTERVALS AND FOR VARIED PURPOSES

In this last case study, Gemma discusses the importance of observing the child at different intervals and for varied purposes.

CASE STUDY 3: GEMMA SIMPSON

Promoting children's progression and supporting their transitions are both areas which I was able to put into practice in the three placement settings attended. Throughout my placement experiences, the technique I adopted from the practitioners prompted me to firstly, observe the children to gauge what they can already achieve independently, then secondly, what they could achieve with support. Following on from this we then plan activities to meet the children's needs and interests. One example from my third placement setting is that the children were extremely interested in sensory rice. From observing this, I planned a sensory rice activity where the children were challenged with the task to trace

(Continued)

(Continued)

some letters from their names in the colourful sensory rice. Planning activities that link to children's interest and individual needs is essential to children's progression. This is because this allows children to engage in activities that they like and have an interest in, an example of child-led learning with the adult as a facilitator.

The adult works as a guide to help and support a young child's development based upon a continuous cycle of observations as can be seen in this case study. The role of the observer is to witness quietly and unobtrusively, to then gather what it is that really interests children, an important skill for all partners within the observation cycle. Research carried out by Fisher (2019) and Howard and McInnes (2012) explains the importance of the adult understanding how the child perceives the activity as one of playfulness. This is an important aspect for your continuing developing practice and one which will require active reflection. Consider asking yourself the following questions:

a.   *How is the child perceiving this activity?*
b.   *What balance have I offered between child led and adult led; have I really planned for the child's interests?*
c.   *What level of motivation and interest is/are the child/ren showing?*

When skilled practitioners work alongside young children a 'collaborative transfer' of knowledge occurs, this enables the child to feel valued; it empowers and supports active learning to take place, an important aspect within the characteristics of effective learning.

Observations within the extract above helped the practitioners to act upon the children's interests and thus fuelled their curiosity and ability to engage and learn (Rogoff, 2003).

COMMENTARY ON CASE STUDY 3

Gemma discusses how she has utilised the children's interests in sensory rice to provide opportunities for the children to engage with mark making. The pedagogical practice of Montessori is drawn upon here, enabling the children to use sensory play experiences to develop the skills necessary for later literacy. Montessori discusses the importance of sensory resources building upon the work of Piaget. Significantly Gemma has recognised the importance of providing the children with a play experience that supports the development of the muscles required for later writing. Consider the importance of this type of activity, perhaps you can engage with some action research using observations that evaluate how effective play opportunities are in supporting both gross and fine motor movement necessary for later writing. Would more opportunities such as these remove the need for pencil grips?

CHILD-LED AND ADULT-LED COMMUNICATION

Competency 4.8 prompts students to explain and demonstrate understanding of the balance between child-led and adult-led activities. As a continuation of this the guidance recognises that 'Children and adults construct the curriculum together. Within the case study Gemma notes: what *they can already achieve independently, then secondly what they could achieve with support.*' This indicates that through careful observation the practitioner can plan to extend the child's learning and development through careful and thoughtful knowledgeable adult interaction. Vygotsky explains this as the more knowledgeable other (MKO). It is interesting to note how Gemma applies this within her planning; therefore, an example of theory being used within practice to extend the opportunities afforded to children, demonstrating how she met Competency 4.2, applying range of observation and research skills to co-construct young children's development, play and learning, encouraging independence and next steps.

For theory to be effective, practitioners must utilise and apply it; therefore, they must have a thorough understanding of how children learn and develop and how theory in-action can support them to enthuse, extend and excite young children through the careful planning of experiences provided to and for the children. The extract highlights the importance of observations within this process.

REFLECTION

Consider Competency 4.7: Identify and apply pedagogical knowledge of how to develop enabling environments indoors and outdoors as you complete the following reflective questions.

Imagine you are in the outdoor environment, and you are observing four children playing. The children are showing curiosity upon seeing their shadows. One of the children notices that their shadow is longer than their friends.

Consider how you would respond and extend the children's learning. What might your next steps be as you build upon the children's interests?

Think about: As you are planning for children's next steps, support your thinking with a theoretical concept (see Figure 4.1).

Observation

Notice the child's play   Listen to the child's voice   Record the interactions that you see

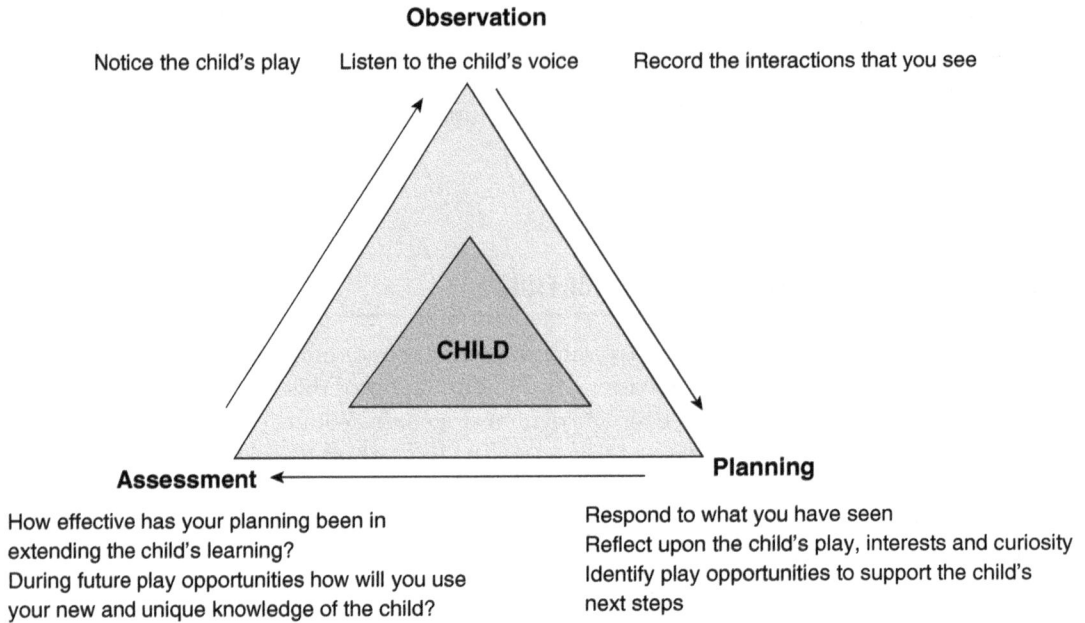

CHILD

Assessment ← **Planning**

How effective has your planning been in extending the child's learning?
During future play opportunities how will you use your new and unique knowledge of the child?

Respond to what you have seen
Reflect upon the child's play, interests and curiosity
Identify play opportunities to support the child's next steps

Figure 4.1   Planning cycle

THE COMPETENCIES IN PRACTICE

The images below show the use of two different methods of observations used in practice (Figures 4.2–4.4).

Settings will independently select to record and undertake observations using differing tools, such as digital, written techniques or other methods. A professional discussion with your mentor/professional partner is a way to familiarise yourself with the methods and techniques used in the setting as you begin to prepare to participate in observing the children.

KNOWLEDGE DEVELOPMENT

The following student extract is taken from a reflective essay that was written to evidence Competency 4.

The Teaching Assistant (TA) asked me if I was able to write observations on her key child because she had noticed that they were spending a lot of time interacting and talking to me. I applied collaborative skills in practice, listened to a TA and worked as part of a team by completing the observations on her key child (ECSDN, 2020). This examples shows that I am being an effective practitioner as I am working collaboratively with the staff in my setting, and that they trust my ability to write

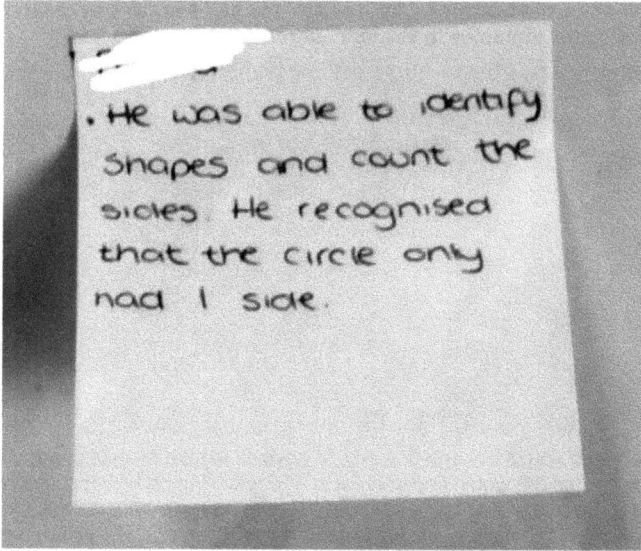

Figure 4.2   Apply a range of observation and research skills to co-construct young children's development, play and learning, encouraging independence and next steps

Observation record sheet

Name of child: E.O.	
Date: 08/04/2022 Time: 9:30 a.m.	
Context of Observation: Phonics lesson	

Notes/Comments	Characteristics of Effective Learning:
E.O. was able to sound out alien words well using fred talk. She was able to blend all the single and special friends sounds presented to her. She is currently reading red ditty books with ease.	**Playing and Exploring Engagement** -Finding out and exploring -Playing with they know -Being willing to 'have a go'
	Active Learning Motivation -Being involved and concentrating -Keep trying -Enjoying achieving what they set out to do
	Creative and Critical Thinking Thinking -Having their own ideas -Making links -Working with ideas
	Prime Areas
	Personal Social and emotional

Figure 4.3   Observation example

Competency 4.10 - Evidence contemporary knowledge and skills in the use of technology and the role and appropriate use of digital literacies in young children's learning. 3-5 years

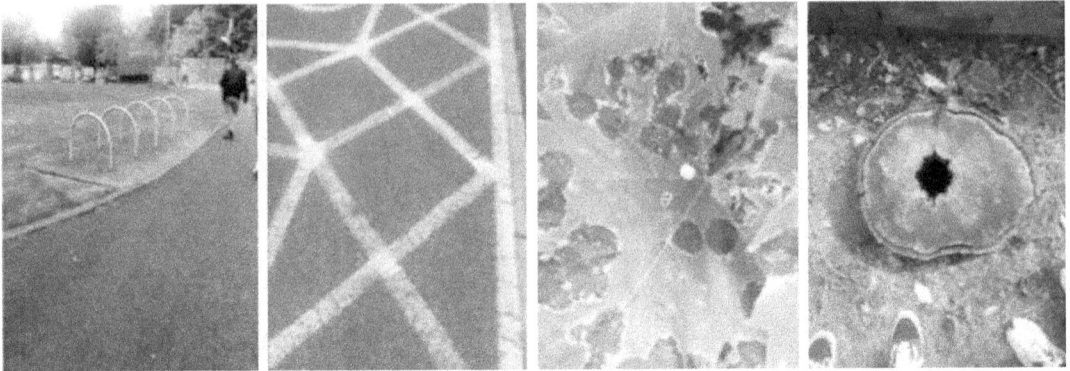

For this session we were to go outdoors and use mobile devices to take images of our surroundings whilst considering what children ages 3-5 would find interest in and reflecting on how technology would be useful to children in this scenario. The use of technology allowed us to bring the outdoors back indoors with us when it came to reflecting on what we had found. I began to realize the advantage of children having accessibility to technology and how it can be used for a positive impact when used appropriately.

The use of technology assists children with their literacy development as the images taken by the children for instance could be incorporated into a themed lesson based on the colours & nature found. This could allow the children to learn an array of new words & associate the outdoors with the new words they have learnt. There were many elements outdoors that also tied in with numeracy skill such as markings on the leaves, shapes that could be seen and symmetry.

Figure 4.4   Example Evidence for Competency 4.10

observations on their key children. The Nutbrown review (2012) suggests that greater learning can be gained from a student becoming part of the community in their setting when on placement, which I am attaining.

Remember, it is imperative that information gathered from observations should be objective, valid and accurate. You can work collaboratively and contribute to peer discussion to compare the use and purpose of observations in early childhood settings. Critically reflect upon the ways observations support you to listen and plan for the child as you prepare for the end point assessment for the ECGPC.

THEORY TO PRACTICE AND PRACTICE TO THEORY

The illustrations and dialogue below highlight links between academic study and vocational experiences forged from experiential lecturer learning.

When we listen to children, truly listen and, take the time to observe, we begin to understand that they are competent co-constructors of the worlds in which they reside (Haeny, Templeton and Nguyen, 2020). The Reggio approach recognises the importance of acknowledging the many diverse ways in which children communicate, thus, enabling many new ways of seeing and therefore the opening of new possibilities, to understand and plan to meet young children's diverse needs and interests (Olsson, 2009). Indeed, when observing, listening and planning for young children, the importance of both community and home is underpinning. As well as the role of nurturing, creative environments in securing both health and well-being, but more importantly young children as confident contributors are key elements within this approach (Rinaldi, 2006). It is, therefore, important to consider the relevance of graduate Competency 4 in relation to the previous statements as it supports the notion that education and care are inseparable, therefore, work hand in hand. In direct contrast, Haeny, Templeton and Nguyen (2020) and Burgess-Macey, Kelly and Ouvry (2020) discuss how in the current neoliberal driven agenda, taking time to reflect and consider the young child's voice is complex and challenging for early childhood professionals. Further, acknowledging the importance of a focus upon what the child can do instead of identifying what they cannot, in an ever more imposed formally driven approach (Burgess-Macey, Kelly and Ouvry, 2020).

Beyond the setting, other stakeholders such as parents and other professionals will be able to offer perspective and insight using their practice, knowledge and professional expertise to contribute to supporting the child's progress. Through the use and purpose of observations in early childhood, shared values are paramount within partnership working. This significantly impacts upon high quality provision and outcomes for children. To support children to become autonomous, curious and learn in their natural environments can be adopted through partnership working. Conkbayir (2021) discusses all that we do in the crucial early years can positively impact upon life trajectories. Upon reflection, Competency 4 supports a deepening awareness of responding to the child's voice through a revisiting of these themes. It will enable you as students or indeed those in practice to navigate the challenges that may be encountered when addressing professional development within the field of Early Childhood Studies at the start and throughout your careers.

CHAPTER SUMMARY

A series of case studies within this chapter have enabled you to examine real-life experiences from a student's perspective within their placements. Competency 4 recognises that when attending work placement, you have a valuable opportunity to observe children in varied contexts, which will then lead you to reflecting and make sense of each child's progress during instantaneous situations. Alongside your professional partners in the setting, you will appreciate the uniqueness of each child in the experiences you observe. Furthermore, this will lead you to integrate spontaneous ways to promote future development and support next steps for children within your role whilst continuing to sustain a child-led approach (Ephgrave, 2018). You will holistically explore all of the nine competencies alongside your academic study making use of these valuable findings from observations to support the progress of each child.

The Early Childhood Studies Degree Network (ECSDN) prompts you to become reflective and reflexive as a highly skilled early years professional. Make use of theory to examine and analyse the implications of your observation findings for practice and developing pedagogical approaches as you further understand the conceptualisation of childhood.

The ECGPC will lead you to gather evidence to reflect your unique and specialist experiences as you complete your academic study and attend placement. Consider the following as you develop your understanding of Competency 4 of the ECGPC.

FURTHER READING

Bradbury, A. and Swailes, R. (2022) *Early Childhood Theories Today*. London: Learning Matters.

Prowle, A. and Hodgkins, A. (2020) *Making a Difference with Children and Families: Re-Imagining the Role of the Practitioner*. London: Bloomsbury Publishing Plc.

Richards, H. and Malomo, M. (eds) (2022) *Developing Your Professional Identity: A Guide for Working with Children and Families*. Critical Publishing.

5

SAFEGUARDING AND CHILD PROTECTION

Caroline Prior

By the end of this chapter, you will be able to:

- Define the key terms 'safeguarding' and 'child protection' with links to legislation and policy.
- Acknowledge the importance of adopting a child-centred approach.
- Review Bronfenbrenner's bio-ecological systems theory model in the context of connecting the child, family and social environment.
- Recognise adverse childhood experiences (ACES) and the implications for multi-agency practice.

KEY TERMS AND DEFINITIONS INCLUDED IN THIS CHAPTER

Early childhood graduate practitioner	**ECGP**
Graduate practitioner competencies	GPCs
Child-centred approach	In safeguarding this involves keeping the child central to all decisions.
Bronfenbrenner's bio-ecological Systems	Bronfenbrenner's theory, the effects of the environment and the quality of relationships on the child's development.
Adverse childhood experiences (ACEs)	The term used to describe stressful events in childhood that can cause long-term health implications.
Multi-agency working	Agencies and professionals working together, co-ordinated intervention to provide support involving sharing information and joint decision-making.
Early help	Adopting a holistic stance offering support in line with family and children needs with the key aim to address any issues in a timely fashion to prevent such issues escalating.

(Continued)

(Continued)

Early childhood graduate practitioner	ECGP
Equal opportunity	A state of fairness, without bias.
Anti-oppressive pedagogical approach	An approach that actively challenges and minimises the effects of oppression in society. For example, anti- racism, anti-classism, anti-sexism.
Socio-economic factors	Factors, such as income, education, employment, community safety, and social network support.

INTRODUCTION

The fundamental principle of safeguarding and child protection involves adopting a child-centred approach that places a child's safety and best interests at the core of high-quality professional practice. Everyone has a responsibility to ensure children feel safe, valued and ultimately protected from harm creating the opportunity for children to thrive and achieve the best outcomes for a healthy and equitable life. Competency 5 looks at safeguarding and child protection of children as outlined below:

COMPETENCY 5: SAFEGUARDING AND CHILD PROTECTION

5.1 Know the wider legislative and statutory guidance for the safeguarding, including child protection, while blowing, digital safety and how these are articulated into the setting policy.

5.2 Recognise when a child may be in danger or at risk of serious harm and the procedures that must be followed.

5.3 Appreciate the importance of working with others to safeguard and promote the well-being of infants and young children.

5.4 Evidence advanced knowledge about child abuse, the wider theoretical perspectives about the causes of abuse and the potential implications for young children's outcomes.

5.5 Apply knowledge of adverse childhood experience, including child abuse to individual planning to promote:
- resilience (including, managing challenge, self-efficacy and self-regulation)
- early learning
- health and well-being
- next steps

5.6 Evidence and apply knowledge and understanding of how globalisation and technology may pose safeguarding risks for young children.

5.7 Know when to signpost to other services or designated persons within the setting to secure young children's safeguarding and protection.

As an early childhood graduate practitioner (ECGP) you have a key role in advocating for children's rights and a statutory responsibility for safeguarding children and their welfare. This chapter explores the key principles of safeguarding and child protection from a practice stance, including how to support you in understanding the complex and multi-faceted components of child abuse and neglect in modern society and your role in working as part of a multi-disciplinary team. The content includes a few reflective activities and University College Birmingham (UCB) ECGP student case study examples to support you in generating ideas for your ECS journey in meeting Competency 5: Creating the opportunity for both personal and professional reflection in recognising the crucial role you must play within the safeguarding and child protection agenda.

DEVELOPING YOUR KNOWLEDGE OF SAFEGUARDING AND CHILD PROTECTION

Developing your knowledge is fundamental and encompasses the need to give every child the security and safety they deserve. So, to begin, it is important to define the key concepts: Safeguarding and Child Protection.

According to the National Society for the Prevention of Cruelty to Children (NSPCC) Learning (2022, para. 2) online platform:

'Safeguarding' is the action that is taken to promote the welfare of children and protect them from harm.

Safeguarding means:

- protecting children from abuse and maltreatment
- preventing harm to children's health or development
- ensuring children grow up with the provision of safe and effective care
- taking action to enable all children and young people to have the best outcomes.

Child protection is part of the safeguarding process. It focuses on protecting individual children identified as suffering or likely to suffer significant harm. This includes child protection procedures which detail how to respond to concerns about a child.

Lumsden (2018) defines safeguarding as a broader term in meeting all children's needs while protecting from harm with child protection aligning to a more generic term involving the need to intervene and protect when there are concerns about a child's safety. Within the concept of safeguarding and multi-agency work, this requires you to be an advocate for the child, family/carer, building trusting and supportive relationships (Walker, 2018).

CHILD PROTECTION FRAMEWORK

The United Kingdom's four nations each have a child protection framework specifying policy and procedures, and it is important that you are familiar with and follow the information relevant to your setting's geographical location.

For example, in England, the Care Act 2014 recognises ten categories of abuse: physical abuse, domestic violence or abuse, sexual abuse, psychological or emotional abuse, financial or material abuse, modern slavery, discriminatory abuse, organisational or institutional abuse with the Wales Safeguarding Procedures recognising the following four forms of abuse: physical, sexual, psychological, emotional alongside key legislation such as the Social Services and Wellbeing (Wales) Act 2014 and the statutory guidance Working Together to Safeguard People (DfE, 2018 – updated 2021).

In Scotland, for anyone working with children the key guidance is the national guidance for child protection in Scotland 2021 and in Northern Ireland the policy document cooperating to safeguard children and young people in Northern Ireland 2017 acts as the overarching principle for this nation.

Each U.K. nation is responsible for its own policies and laws; they are all based on the similar principles within the child protection agenda:

- protecting children from abuse and maltreatment
- preventing harm to children's health or development
- ensuring children grow up with the provision of safe and effective care
- taking action to enable all children and young people to have the best outcomes.

(NSPCC, 2022, para 2)

For the purposes of this chapter, the content will review the child protection systems in England.

CASE STUDY 1: LEGISLATION AND STATUTORY GUIDANCE

The following case study shows how ECGP students discussed and created a mind map demonstrating their **knowledge of the wider legislative and statutory guidance for the safeguarding including child protection, whistle blowing, digital safety and how these are articulated into setting policy (5.1).** *They discussed implications for their graduate practice including the need for continuing professional development (CPD).*

Remember to consider any updates to statutory frameworks in line with your period of study and geographical location. For example, the keeping children safe in education 2022 applicable to England has since been revised following completion of this activity, and it is important you adopt a constant CPD stance to ensure your knowledge and practice remains current.

Further ECGP student discussion explored **knowledge and understanding of how globalisation and technology may pose safeguarding risks for young children (5.6)**, recognising how engagement in online platforms has increased for young children and the need for setting safeguarding policies to reflect this (Figures 5.1 and 5.2).

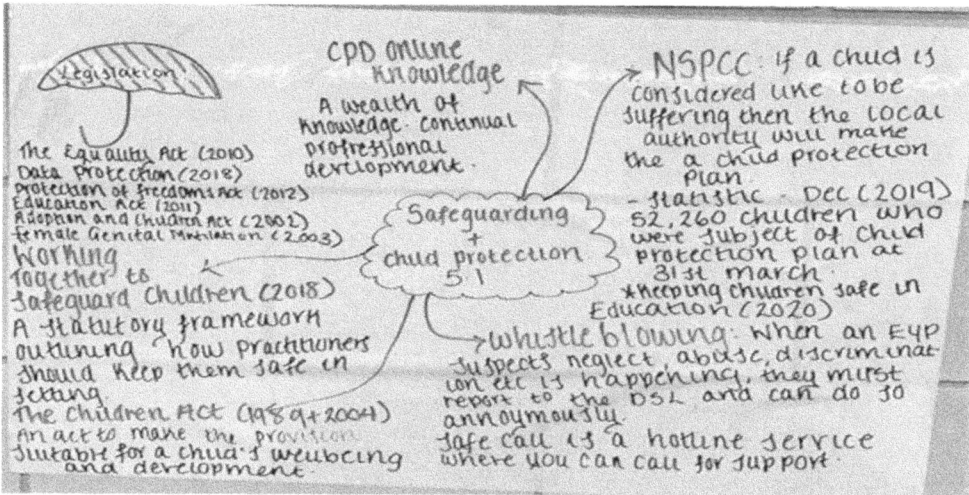

Figure 5.1 Mindmaps illustrating knowledge of competency

REFLECTION

Recognising when a child may be in danger or at risk
Take some time to pause and reflect. Consider the following questions to support your graduate practice *in recognising when a child may be in danger or at risk of serious harm and the procedures that must be followed (5.2)*:

- How are you going to ensure your knowledge of government legislative and statutory requirements is current?
- How will you identify how these are articulated into setting policy demonstrating critical links between your knowledge and professional practice for your GPC evidence?
- Where can you access your setting's policies? When was the last time you read the policies and procedures? For example, child protection policy, behaviour policy (including measures to prevent bullying, cyberbullying, prejudice-based and discriminatory bullying), staff behaviour policy?
- Do you understand the role of, and who, the designated safeguarding lead (DSL) is at your setting? If not, where will you find this information?

Compose a list of personal action points. For example, ensure you attend a full induction at your setting, embrace on going continuing professional development, for example, UCB students accessed free online ACE training and then included the certificate for GPC evidence in their portfolio.

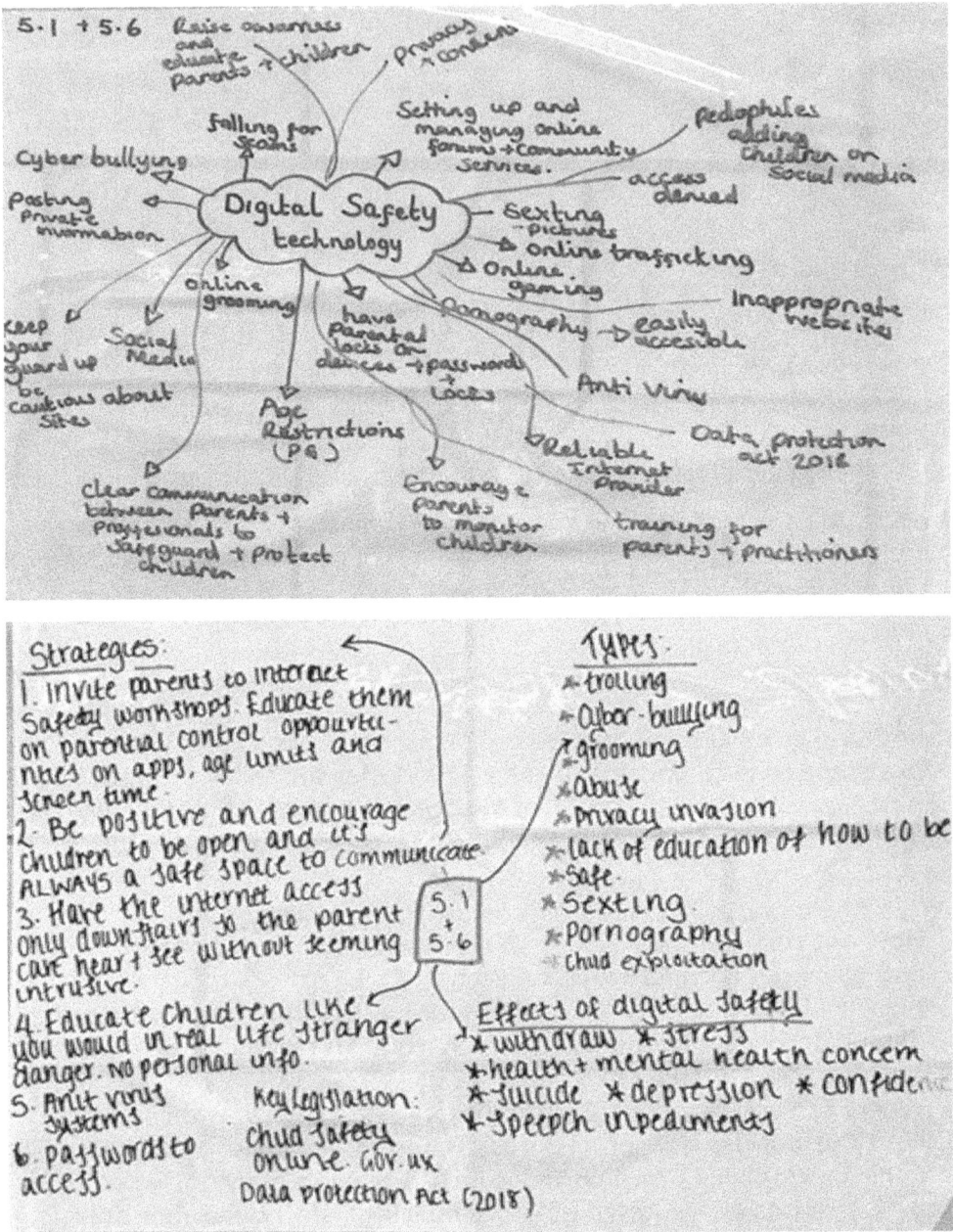

Figure 5.2   Mindmaps illustrating knowledge of competency

REFLECTION

How safeguarding is demonstrated in practice

- Consider how safeguarding policies are articulated into setting policy (5.1) as part of your early years and/or school setting experience.

(Continued)

(Continued)

- Consider all aspects of the provision ensuring a child-centred approach including opportunities to involve parents/carers in working with others to safeguard and promote the well-being of infants and young children (Figure 5.3).
- To develop, add further comments justifying why these elements are important in support of critical reflection.
- Can you include secure links between statutory frameworks and effective safeguarding and child protection practice to support this?

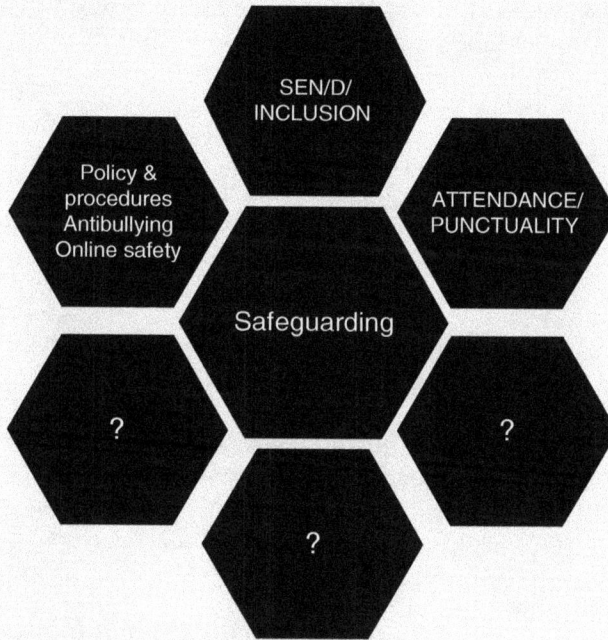

Figure 5.3 Activity reflecting on the 'why'

CHILD ABUSE AND NEGLECT

It is important that you define the key term *child abuse* considering your own values and beliefs and how these may impact on your thoughts and ultimately your professional practice. Wilson (2016) discusses how reflecting upon personal values is an in-depth essential component of graduate practice requiring honesty and objectivity and whereby our own experiences help us make sense of the world they can act as potential cognitive barriers especially when family practices or beliefs differ from our own.

REFLECTION

- How would you define child abuse?
- What has influenced your answer? Think about personal experiences and values, study experiences including professional expectations and any wider influences.

Adopting an on going highly reflective stance, taking time to review your personal values and how these may have an impact on your professional identity is crucial to recognising how you construct your thoughts and how these drive your professional behaviour especially within the concept of safeguarding and child protection. You need to acknowledge the complexities of society, leading to a range of complex family situations requiring the adoption of a non-judgemental disposition, while adhering to required safeguarding and child protection policy and procedure.

Case Study 2 is an exercise presented to ECGP students. The scenario was reviewed using the reflective questions, while considering their role in line with the setting's safeguarding policy and the role of the designated safeguarding lead in recognising when a child may be in danger or at risk of serious harm and the procedures to follow (5.2).

CASE STUDY 2

Recognising when a child may be in danger or at risk of serious harm and the procedures to follow (5.2)

Scenario

Kelly and Jake are married with two children Destiny, four years, and Francesca, six years.

Both parents have a history of heroin use and both continue to inject heroin even though they are on methadone treatment with Jake having been in prison previously for drug-related crimes. Both parents are not working and claim benefits. The family have been involved in the social care system intermittently over the past few years.

Jake experienced abuse as a child, and was involved in the social care system, from a young age. Kelly has mild learning difficulties, has limited contact with her extended family and support networks.

The family live in a high rise flat and have been allocated a floating support worker who has worked with them for the last six months.

Jake is well-known to housing staff for his volatile nature and frequent verbally abusive calls to centre staff. As the case study unfolds, multiple issues become apparent, i.e. anti-social behaviour, alcohol abuse, mental health issues, adverse childhood experiences (ACEs) and drug abuse.

Destiny and Francesca are both at school, but their attendance is erratic and recently the school has raised concerns that Kelly is often late collecting the children from school and sometimes appears intoxicated.

Destiny's speech and language is very poor, and she sometimes smells strongly of urine when she comes to school. Francesca is showing behaviour

(Continued)

(Continued)

problems at school; sometimes she becomes very angry and sometimes is quiet and withdrawn.

Both children appear unclean, tired and find it hard to concentrate.

REFLECTION

- Do you think this is abuse? If so, can you identify the types of abuse?
- What may be some of the factors causing concern for this family?
- Discuss potential concerns and needs across each family member ensuring they have considered what the family needs.
- What may be the long-term impact on the children? Family?
- What would you do?

Often the concept of child abuse is viewed as challenging and complex due to a range of influencing factors such as cultural practices, societal views and political intervention. Abuse is often deemed as socially constructed (Lumsden, 2018) and society is constantly changing at an ever-increasing speed, for example, consider the impact of technology and access to the internet. We know there are many positives to children using technology such as promoting independence and empowerment, but due to the evolving landscape children are now facing further cyberbullying threats involving racism and physical harm (McAFee, 2022). Consider the impact of the global pandemic and how this has adversely affected many children and families in different ways and is continuing to do so. Socio-economic factors and health factors including mental health add to the complexities of the safeguarding agenda and how or what constitutes child abuse. Could we, therefore, argue that a static definition is not feasible? However, there needs to be a working definition and we could agree that the inclusion of the term intentional harm is non-negotiable (Figure 5.4).

Child abuse is when a child is intentionally harmed by an adult or another child – it can be over a period of time but can also be a one-off action. It can be physical, sexual or emotional and it can happen in person or online. It can also be a lack of love, care and attention – this is neglect.

(NSPCC, 2022)

Table 5.1 gives a brief overview of four types of abuse as defined by the Department of Education in England developed to incorporate such aspects as cyberbullying and online grooming in line with societal change. Domestic abuse has also been added to the list of safeguarding issues that all staff should be aware of.

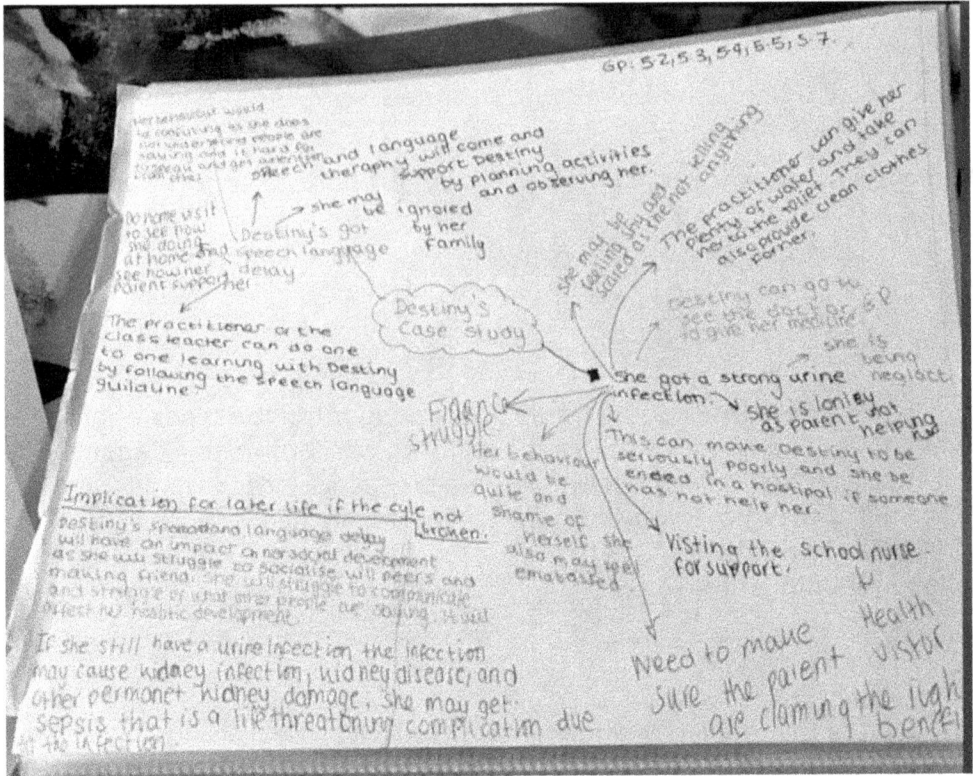

Figure 5.4 Mindmap showing response to case study about destiny

UNDERSTANDING AND IDENTIFYING ABUSE AND NEGLECT

Understanding and identifying the types of abuse is crucial, and although Table 5.1 gives an overview of the main categories, it is important to research wider influences on the family and child to support you understanding the range of difficulties often faced due to the complexities of human interactions and relationships, behaviour, cultural norms and the impact of the environment and political ideologies.

Bronfenbrenner's (1979, 1992, 2005) bio-ecological systems theory identifies a range of complex factors connecting the child, family and social environment including the concept of continuity and change in the bio-psychological characteristics of human beings, both as individuals and as groups. Bronfenbrenner maintains that the individual develops within context, and that human development is a systematic approach to human and social development. The relationships children have with parents/carers can impact their development and in return, these relationships are affected by parents'/carers' experiences in their work and community settings, which are also affected by broader social, cultural and policy conditions. A useful theoretical model to support you in understanding how events can affect families and children depicting human development as a transactional process, which in return highlights form a safeguarding stance the need for multi-agency working, a statutory requirement of the Children Act 1989 strengthened by the Children

Table 5.1 Indicators of abuse and neglect

Abuse	A form of maltreatment of a child. Somebody may abuse or neglect a child by inflicting harm or by failing to act to prevent harm. Harm can include ill treatment that is not physical as well as the impact of witnessing ill treatment of others. This can be particularly relevant, for example, in relation to the impact on children of all forms of domestic abuse.
	Abuse can take place wholly online, or technology may be used to facilitate offline abuse or children.
Physical abuse	A form of abuse which may involve hitting, shaking, throwing, poisoning, burning or scalding, drowning, suffocating or otherwise causing physical harm to a child.
Emotional abuse	The persistent emotional maltreatment of a child such as to cause severe and adverse effects on the child's emotional development.
Sexual abuse	Involves forcing or enticing a child or young person to take part in sexual activities, not necessarily involving violence, whether or not the child is aware of what is happening.
Neglect	The persistent failure to meet a child's basic physical and/or psychological needs, likely to result in the serious impairment of the child's health or development.

Keeping Children Safe in Education 2022 Part one: Safeguarding information for all staff. Points 26 – 30

Act 2004. Agencies are required to proactively collaborate placing the child's well-being at the core, in other words, creating systems that support both the child and the family (Walker, 2018).

BRONFENBRENNER'S (1979, 1992, 2005) BIO-ECOLOGICAL SYSTEMS THEORY

However, one of the criticisms of Bronfenbrenner's theoretical model is that whereby the model recognises the negative influences of adversity and trauma on an individual, it fails to recognise the importance of developing resilience and the role this plays in supporting individuals in overcoming negative environmental experiences (Christensen, 2016) (Figures 5.5 and 5.6).

Grimmer (2021, 2022) applies Bronfenbrenner's model to the concept of empowering children through adopting a loving pedagogy. By adopting an interconnected holistic approach placing the child at the core, you can ensure that your graduate practice continues to offer advocacy and agency to the child and family involving key aspects of valuing, including them and listening to their views. Furthermore, quality parent–child interaction in the context of the family relationships supports children to develop social understanding and self-regulation, crucial for holistic development, social well-being and life success (Robson and Zachariou, 2022). The development of trusting relationships between you, as the graduate practitioner, and all parents/carers create opportunities to support and share information, and where applicable signposting parents/carers to more targeted interventions such as parenting programmes (Wilson, 2016).

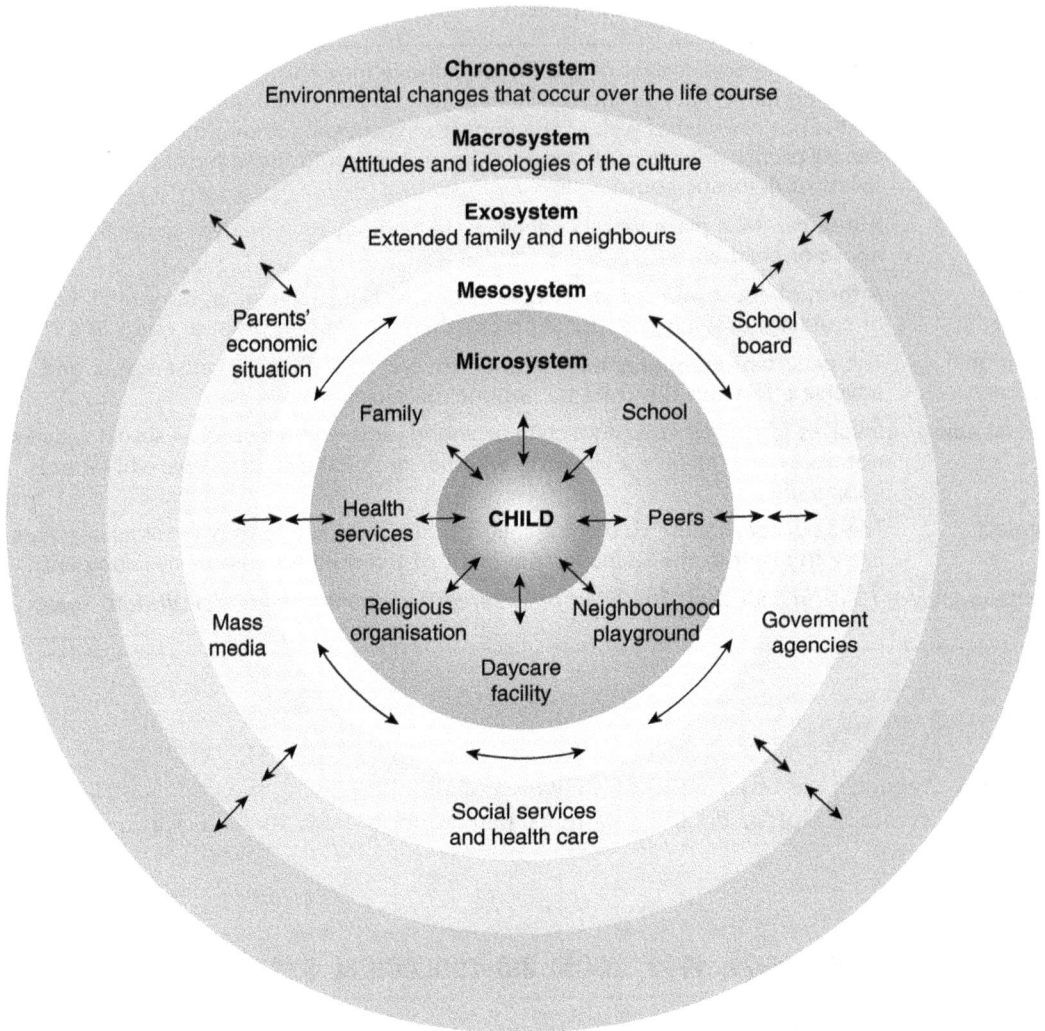

Figure 5.5   Bronfenbrenner' bio-ecological systems theory (1979, 1992, 2005)

REFLECTION

Recognising the importance of quality relationships
    Consider Bronfenbrenner's bio-ecological model and the importance of quality relationships. Can you critically apply this theory to your graduate practice?

    Review the following questions to support your reflection:

(Continued)

(Continued)

- How do you maintain quality relationships with the children/parents/carers?
- Can you use this model to explore why children may behave differently at Nursery/school from home?
- What may be *wider theoretical perspectives about the causes of abuse (5.4)* including potential factors that can affect a child and family? How can you support from a practice stance?

In relation to one of the criticisms of this model, can you develop your reflection to consider:

- What is resilience and why is this concept important?
- How do you support children/parents in developing resilience?
- How does the above fit into your safeguarding responsibilities?

It is important to recognise at this time that **resilience (including managing challenge, self-efficacy and self-regulation)** is an important protective factor that helps children and families cope with difficulties and stresses in their lives in meeting **Competency 5.5.**

ADVERSE CHILDHOOD EXPERIENCES (ACES)

According to the Center on the Developing Child (2019), adverse childhood experiences (ACEs) are factors such as physical and emotional abuse, neglect and a range of contributing factors such as poverty, mental health difficulties, racism and domestic violence. The responses to and effects of such adversities can lead to toxic stress affecting a child's development, and academic achievement. The negative effects can potentially lead to long-term health conditions such as diabetes, substance abuse and heart conditions ultimately affecting a child's life outcomes. ACEs can affect families and children across all social levels with the First 1,000 Days Movement, campaigning for the importance of emotional well-being in babies and this stage acting as a crucial window of opportunity in securing the best possible outcomes across all aspects of life (Parent-Infant Foundation, 2022).

Lumsden (2018) discusses the concept of ACEs from a child abuse stance and reinforces the effects of a child living within stressful environments with the need for interventions to break the cycle of adversity within family units. However, that said she continues to advocate that there are no quick remedies as some families require on going support within a nurturing and child-responsive environment.

REFLECTION

Adverse Childhood Experiences (ACEs)
Carry out some further research to support your **knowledge of adverse childhood experience** considering the following points:

- How can the ECGP support? Think about the key term resilience within the previous activity.
- What strategies did you consider in support of your graduate practice? What are the theoretical links to your answer?

Examples could include secondary attachment and developing secure attachment through play (Moore, 2022).
Consider the role parents/carers have and how children require them to provide a secure base (Lumsden, 2018).

- What may be some of the potential wider issues affecting the family unit?
- How can you support parents/carers?

We cannot be expected to solve all issues as we are not qualified/equipped to do so, and this is where the key term *collaboration* comes in. Working with others is also known as *integrated working* (Lumsden, 2018) (see Chapters 3, 7 and 8).

EARLY HELP AGENDA

Early help cannot claim to resolve every situation, but it is viewed as essential in minimising the effects of such entities as economic disadvantage, supporting social mobility and ultimately improving children's life chances (Early Intervention Foundation, 2023) with intervention actioned at the right time proving to be effective (Center on the Developing Child, 2019).

The Government's statutory guidance, Working Together to Safeguard Children (DFE, 2018) under Chapter 1: Assessing need and providing help with a subheading entitled Identifying children and families who would benefit from early help recognising the need for multi-agency training and practitioners being best placed to identify triggers and symptoms of abuse, shares concerns and offer children appropriate support whilst recognising their commitment to continual professional development in keeping abreast of key changes and 'new and emerging threats' (Powell, 2019). The Keeping Children Safe in Education statutory guidance updated in September 2002 places importance on a child-centred and coordinated approach to safeguarding reinforcing the role of the ECGP in practice and working as part of a multi-disciplinary team. Ultimately, early help services aim to prevent problems from escalating taking on board a holistic view regarding the child and family's wider needs.

Competency 5.7 asks you to 'Know *when to signpost to other services or designated persons within the setting to secure young children's safeguarding and protection'.*

It is important to ensure your practice is informed by knowledge of available services and appropriate assessment procedures. Consider links between the Equality Act 2010 and safeguarding reflecting on how this is demonstrated in your professional practice. Bradbury (2022) discusses the work of Dr Valerie Daniel, a Maintained Nursery School Executive Head Teacher, and how she adopts a continual anti-oppressive pedagogical approach signifying the importance of inclusive practices fully embedded in everyday practice and not being considered in isolation.

LEVEL OF NEED AND ASSESSMENT

Under the Children Act 2004, amended by the Children and Social Work Act 2017, Local Safeguarding Children Boards, set up by local authorities, were replaced by a team of safeguarding partners to work collaboratively to strengthen the child protection and safeguarding system: local authorities, chief officers of police and clinical commissioning groups (Working Together to Safeguard Children, 2018).

The Children Act 1989 Section 17 defines a child in need as unlikely to reach or maintain a satisfactory level of health or development, or their health and development will be significantly impaired without the provision of services, or children who are disabled or at risk of significant harm, as outlined in Section 47 of the Children Act 1989. Therefore, it is crucial to determine the level of need or risk, to help determine an appropriate response.

Any assessment needs to take a holistic child-centred approach rooted in child development with a focus on action that secures the best possible outcomes, while embracing equal opportunity and a transparent approach by working in partnership with parents (Walker, 2018). Bradbury (2022) adds that early childhood graduates need to be aware of the holistic needs of the child and family and the significant barriers some may face highlighting the importance of developing trustful relationships with the family.

The following case study shows an example of a family scenario to explore the level of need and services required.

CASE STUDY 4: LEVELS OF NEED

Luca is four years old and has been attending the setting very sporadically for three months. You have been monitoring Luca since he started due to concerns around his attendance, appearance and constant hunger when in Nursery. Luca is a quiet child and seems to do his best not to be noticed. You have spoken with his mother previously about this and she always has an excuse, for example, slept in so did not have time for breakfast or the washing machine is broken.

Today Luca comes into Nursery and as usual is hungry, looks tired, dirty and unkempt. His mother says once again that they overslept.

You make Luca some breakfast and sit with him to ask if he had a nice weekend, Luca becomes upset and says, 'Mummy said I can't tell you'. You comfort Luca and ask if he would like to tell you anything.

Luca tells you that on the weekend 'big men' came into his house and took some of mummy's stuff because she had no money. He also tells you his house is always dark and cold, and he has no food.

REFLECTION

Consider the following reflective questions:

- What are the predisposing factors within the case study and level of support needed?

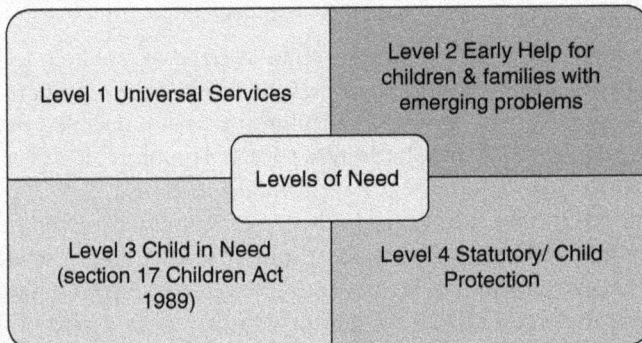

Figure 5.6   Levels of need

(Continued)

(Continued)

- Carry out research to determine the levels of need in the table below. For example, what services sit under the *Universal* umbrella?
- What may be the potential implications for the child's development/future outcomes?
- How would you support Luca and his mother within your daily practice?
- Examples of external support services?

CHAPTER SUMMARY

This chapter provides an introduction to Competency 5: Safeguarding and Child Protection; however, due to the complexities of this topic, the content should not be viewed in isolation and independent reading and research in support of your on going professional development and/or academic study is strongly advised.

Being an advocate for shaping a child's future and securing better outcomes requires passion and dedication placing you, as a highly knowledgeable and skilled ECGP at the forefront of graduate practice. The case studies and reflective activities are designed to support your knowledge and the critical application of this knowledge to your graduate practice in meeting the value-added addition of the GPCs promoting empowerment, protection and independence for all children and families.

FURTHER READING

Frost, N. (2020) *Safeguarding Children and Young People: A Guide for Professionals Working Together.* London: Sage Publications Ltd.

Lumsden, E. (2018) *Child Protection in the Early Years. A Practical Guide.* London: Jessica Kingsley Publishers.

Munro, E. (2019) *Effective Child Protection.* London: Sage Publications Ltd.

USEFUL WEBSITES

https://learning.nspcc.org.uk/newsletter/caspar
    The NSPCC FREE weekly email newsletter for practice, policy and research to keep you up-to-date with all the latest safeguarding and child protection news. The CASPAR briefings help people working or volunteering with children and young people understand changes to safeguarding and child protection

https://foundationyears.org.uk/2019/08/safeguarding/
    Foundation Years. A free hub of national safeguarding resources to empower children, young people and all adults supporting them

https://www.safeguardingresourcehub.co.uk/
    Safeguarding Resource Hub: a free hub of national safeguarding resources to empower children, young people and all adults supporting them.

https://earlyyearsreviews.co.uk/
    Early Years Reviews. Current early years and education topics.

6

INCLUSIVE PRACTICE

Debbie Nye and *Helen Perkins*

CHAPTER ACKNOWLEDGEMENTS

With thanks to the following students and practitioners for their contributions:
Mubshara Bakar and Elizabeth Dunning

> **By the end of this chapter, you will be able to:**
>
> - Explore the complex dimensions of inclusive practice and its impact on children and their families.
> - Demonstrate the application of knowledge about inclusive practice, including how these relate to your graduate practitioner competencies.
> - Engage with the literature and legislation relating to inclusive practice to understand how inclusion is underpinned by regulation.
> - Demonstrate the ability to apply theory to inclusive practice when collating gathering evidence for your graduate practitioner competencies.

KEY TERMS AND DEFINITIONS INCLUDED IN THIS CHAPTER

Inclusion	Inclusion is a process of identifying, understanding and breaking down barriers to participation and belonging
Protected characteristics	Age, disability, gender reassignment, race, religion or belief, sex, sexual orientation, marriage and civil partnership
Equality	Fairness through treating everyone the same regardless of need
Equity	Treating people differently dependent on need
Prejudice	Preconceived opinion that is not based on reason or actual experience

(Continued)

(Continued)

Discrimination	Discrimination is when someone is treated unfairly based on the group, class or category to which they are perceived to belong
Race	The term 'race' refers to a person's physical appearance, such as skin colour, eye colour and hair colour. It refers to the division of people into populations or groups based on various sets of physical characteristics
Ethnicity	Ethnicity relates to cultural factors such as nationality, culture, ancestry, language and beliefs
Disability	Any condition that makes it more difficult for a person to do certain activities or have equitable access to the world around them
Special Educational Needs and Disability SEND	There are four broad areas of SEND: Communication and Interaction Cognition and Learning Social Emotional and/or Mental Health Physical and/or Sensory
Unconscious bias	Unconscious favouritism towards or prejudice against people of a particular race, ethnicity religion, gender or social group that influences one's actions or perceptions
SENCO	Special educational needs coordinator – Person responsible for assessing, planning and monitoring the progress of children with special educational needs and disabilities
LGBTQ+	Lesbian, gay, bisexual, transgender, queer (or sometimes questioning) and others. The 'plus' represents other sexual identities including pansexual and Two-Spirit
Unique Child	A unique child is an active agent of their own development. Development from pre-birth into early childhood, progression is uneven and unfolds differently for each individual child
Reflective practice	The act of applying critical evaluative thinking to practice or behaviour.
Reflexive practice	Be self-aware about the motivations for focusing on the area of research or practice

INTRODUCTION

We live in a diverse society, in which some groups of people are marginalised and experience discrimination, impacting on their education, health and long-term life chances. As an early childhood graduate practitioner, it is essential that you encourage children to notice the many aspects of diversity, in doing so you can create a positive approach to inclusion and have a lasting impact on society. This chapter will explore the concept of Competency 6, inclusive practice, through the lens of the 'Unique child (DfE, 2021a)'. We will include the broader definition of inclusion, considering the protected characteristics, identified in the Equality Act,

2010, age, disability, gender reassignment, race, religion or belief, sex, sexual orientation, marriage and civil partnership.

COMPETENCY 6: INCLUSIVE PRACTICE

6.1   Evidence knowledge, understanding and application in practice of pedagogy that supports inclusion.

6.2   Know how to identify infants and young children who may require additional support and how to refer to appropriate services.

6.3   Demonstrate an understanding of statutory guidance for children with special educational needs and disabilities and protected characteristics.

6.4   Evidence skills in appropriate planning to address the care and early learning needs of individual young children with special educational needs and/or disabilities and protected characteristics.

The case studies will highlight the importance of representation for both children and their families. Examples from students' portfolios are shared to demonstrate how they met Competency 6, Inclusive practice. The discussion following each case study will assist you in building your knowledge and skills in terms of inclusive practice and the reflective questions will challenge you to consider your personal values and beliefs and to develop your personal pedagogy.

THE CONTEXT OF INCLUSION LEGISLATION AND REGULATION

Legislation relating to inclusion in the United Kingdom has been evolving since the 1960s. As a deeper understanding of the long-term effects of discrimination within a person's life course (particularly about childhood) developed, the complex nature of difference became the focus of legislation. The Race Relations Act 1965 was the first legislation in the United Kingdom to address racial discrimination on the 'grounds of colour, race, or ethnic or national origins'. Inclusion for children with special educational needs began with the Warnock Report in 1978 (HMSO, 1978); this was the first legislative focus which made local authorities responsible for meeting their needs by regular assessment and review. Sexual equality legislation for LQBTQ+ is more complicated. For example, up until 1967, homosexuality was a criminal offence in England (being gay is still a criminal offence in many parts of the world). Gay sex remained illegal in Scotland and Northern Ireland until 1982, while transgender people were not protected in equality legislation until 2010 (please do take some time to research the timeline for legislation in your home nation). The Equality Act (2010) combined the many and disparate pieces of legislation into one Act, identifying several protected characteristics that are considered in law to be at risk of discrimination or marginalisation. The Act provides the legal framework necessary to uphold people's rights and advance opportunity and equality for all.

Competency 6 should be evidenced throughout your portfolio, giving examples from practice, demonstrating your developing knowledge and understanding of inclusion. It should inform ethical practices and be threaded throughout all the other competencies.

The case studies, shared from a student's perspective, will enable you to make connections between theory, legislation, practice and academic study. As in other chapters, the content is underpinned by reference to the Birth to 5 Matters (The Early Years Coalition, 2021) and the Early Years Foundation Stage (DfE, 2021a) theme of 'the unique child'. There are reflective questions for you to work through to develop your understanding of inclusive practice and your role as a graduate practitioner and to stimulate ideas for evidencing how you are meeting the ECGPC.

IDENTIFYING CHILDREN WHO MAY REQUIRE ADDITIONAL SUPPORT

The first case study is an extract from the student's oral assessment which centres on identifying children who may require additional support and how to refer them to appropriate services (Graduate Competency 6.2). Mushaira (student graduate practitioner) understood that every school and Early Years setting should have a safeguarding officer, as well as a special educational needs and disability coordinator. She had developed a good relationship with them and was able to keep up-to-date with the children in her group. She knew to contact them if she has any concerns about a child.

CASE STUDY 1

I had a child, who had just moved to the United Kingdom, and he doesn't know any English, but he does use his home language. This made communication difficult; I could understand bits of what he said and the same for him as our home languages had similarities, but he still struggled. I thought about how I could help him and spoke to his mum. Mum bought in some pictures of his family and at home suggesting this may help. I thought this was a great idea and created a board for him to use (ECGPC 6.4).

I then remember discussing PECS (Picture Exchange Communication System) at university, so I created a set of pictures to help him communicate better; every child is good at learning. I found pictures, cartoons and photographs (ECGPC 6.1). I printed out images like the toilet, the kitchen, outdoors and home and underneath I wrote the words in English and his mum added the home language. So that way, not only is he going to slowly learn from the image, but he can still value the use of his home language as he names the picture. I could also repeat the English word to him when he pointed to each picture and, you know, he'll learn to understand what's written on it. So that was like a sense of interaction, even though he's not able to speak the language but at least he's understanding the images. I had regular meetings with the teacher, safeguarding and special educational needs coordinator (SENCo) about this child. I spoke to the safeguarding officer (his language barrier had to be monitored as a concern due to not being able to tell us if anything had happened or he needed

(Continued)

(Continued)

help) and the SENCo, and they helped me to make plans to help him progress further (ECGPC 6). We would set weekly targets for me to work on with him to help him develop his English and start to communicate with others in the class. Slowly he started to learn the basic words, and this led to him beginning to socialise with the others. The language I had shared with him on the PECS board helped him to start simple conversations that interaction with other children went on to help him develop further. Eventually, he no longer needed the PECS or the close work with me or the supporting team.

COMMENTARY ON CASE STUDY 1

As suggested in the case study, children sometimes face challenges (developmental) or marginalisation when circumstances change, it is important to identify quickly where a child needs additional support as barriers to communication affect the child and the family's engagement in all aspects of the child's education and care (Early Years Coalition, 2021). The student reflected on the situation through the child's lens and was able to understand the challenges. She spoke with the family, and it was that interaction that led her to introduce the PECS system, 'Creating an ethos of equality involves being aware of how all the practices and environments in an early year setting appear through the lens of each unique child' (Early Years coalition, 2021, p. 24) (ECGPC 6.1). The Childcare Act (2006) requires you to report any concerns to the setting SENCo, safeguarding officer and your manager. Referral may then be made that will involve multi-agency working and professionals specifically trained in areas of concern (see Competencies 3, 5 and 8). The student engaged with the teacher, safeguarding designated member of staff and the SENCo to enable her to verify her ideas for support, monitor progress and plan for future steps (ECGPC 6.2). She also gave scope to continue to use, and value the child's home language alongside learning English. This supported the child to feel welcome and gain a sense of belonging which is essential to the child's well-being and impacts on their ability to learn. Engaging with the family, bringing pictures and artefacts can make connections across environments, providing an anchor for them and their learning. It was important to provide this additional support as 'Communication and language lay a foundation for learning and development, guiding and supporting children's thinking while underpinning their emerging literacy' (2021, p. 44). The student continued to engage with the professionals to enable progress and further planning, but equally highlighting any further intervention or support needed.

Our culture, beliefs and biases are frequently so subtle that we are unaware of their impact on how we interact and behave (Lynch and Hanson, 2004). Practitioners themselves carry a wealth of knowledge from their own diverse backgrounds that should be celebrated (Birth to Five Matters, 2021). The student used her own experience of having English as an Additional Language to support the child and the family.

REFLECTION

- Reflect upon the importance of working with parents when supporting children with English as an Additional Language, what are the challenges and opportunities?
- Reflect on your pedagogy, how would you support this child and his family?
- Consider the whole child, what potential challenges to inclusion might they experience?

A CHILD WITH AUTISM

This extract focuses on Lizzy's experiences. She is a student practitioner in a private Nursery attached to a school taking two- to three-year-olds she is a level 5 student.

CASE STUDY 2

We have a little boy in our setting, and he is currently being assessed for autism. His parents are at the early stages of coming to terms with the possibility and are still unsure what the future holds. He is only three, he'll be starting nursery school this year. We have observed him on his arrival in the setting and again for the referral and have noted his main interest are dinosaurs. He tended to stay in the small world corner and only play with the dinosaurs and if they were not out, he would ask for them. Because I know that he needs support in some areas, through planning and assessment, I become aware of where he needs more help to build his knowledge and skills, but also, you want to broaden his experiences so that he can develop his socialisation and relationships. So, I used the dinosaurs to encourage him to move around and explore the setting, I put the dinosaurs in construction. I sat with him, and we built a house. He is quite sensory averse and really didn't like the sand, water, or other sensory activities and it took a good six months but now he happily plays with the dinosaurs in the sand and water. But it's about the knowledge that is given to planning with the child's interests in mind. So, by bringing the dinosaurs into the sand, we built a tunnel in the sand. I had attended 'Schema Play' training I recognised what I was doing is 'seeding' resources to encourage the child to engage and stretch and challenge his play, creating a lot of scope to cover all areas of his development (Siraj-Blatchford and Brock, 2016).

(Continued)

(Continued)

I started by parallel playing with him, playing at his side and slowly I began to interact with him until he responded. With autism, his responses could be different to other children, and he did exhibit anxiety through the interaction but with lots of reassurance through the play, he began to relax. Once I felt he was secure in this and it took several weeks, I introduced another child and in turn worked with him on that interaction until I was able to step back, and others joined. It is a gentle process with autism, and it does depend on the child's particular traits which are different in every child but, it is about getting to know your children and building your activities and responses around that relationship with the knowledge.

COMMENTARY ON CASE STUDY 2

The case study demonstrates the support given to a child, possibly with a special educational need or disability (SEND) who has been identified as needing extra support. The procedures have been followed for referral but while awaiting a response the student, with the support of the setting SENCo, is introducing strategies learned in lectures, to plan for and support the child. The planning is essential to this process; the child has been assessed and monitored before the referral was made to provide the evidence behind the recommendation, 'on-going assessment should help practitioners discover in more detail the factors influencing the child's learning and development' (DfE, 2021, p. 15). The SENCo is pivotal in the overview of the child's progress, ensuring that all communications are disseminated and acted upon. Observations are also used in the setting to establish further interventions that will support the scaffolding of the child's learning while maintaining a good level of self-efficacy (ECGPC: 6.4, 4.2 and 4.7).

The student introduced two key strategies during this time, the first was to observe him and notice his key interests as Birth to 5 Matters suggests 'on-going formative assessment is at the heart of effective early years practice' (The Early Years Coalition, p. 38). In turn, this enabled her to use this knowledge to encourage the child to engage with other activities within the setting. This will over time not only stretch and challenge his learning but increase his self-esteem, confidence and sense of belonging in the setting.

The second key intervention she initiated was to introduce him to be comfortable with other children around him during play. Children whose development is different may not develop a sense of belonging. Developing his play will help with his socialisation within the group and empower him in activity situations. Parten (1933) emphasised the idea that learning to play is learning how to relate to others, unlike Piaget (1962) who saw types of play in primarily cognitive developmental terms.

As a protected characteristic (ECGPC 6.3) under the Equality Act (2010) this is particularly of relevance for children with autism, as one of the many key characteristics can struggle with social interaction and communication (National Autistic Society, 2022). For this reason, some children with autism may find it hard to form friendships; they may want to interact with other people and make friends but may be unsure how to go about it. So the practitioner is working closely with the child to develop his skills in an area that could be very challenging for him and may need support. It is also an integral part of preparing for school. The progress made, as a level five student, is evidenced in the developing quality of interaction and successful outcomes of her interventions. When working with children with special educational needs and disabilities (SEND) practitioners 'should acknowledge and value each child, emphasising what they can do through a strengths-based perspective on disability (The Early Years Coalition, p. 27) emphasising the importance of the unique Child'.

The United Nations Convention on the Rights of the Child (UNCRC) (UNICEF, 1989) states that a child with a disability has the right to live a full life with dignity and independence to play an active part in the community. Birth to 5 Matters (Early Years Coalition, 2021) states that children with SEN receive extra support through inclusive practice in the setting, resulting in better outcomes for children.

REFLECTION

- How could you use the UNCRC and Birth to 5 Matters to effectively support a child's early learning and progression? (Comp: 6.1, 6.3)
- Divergent development may be viewed as a deficit, observe the language used when discussing children with a SEND, how might these terms affect the child's experiences. Rephrase negative terms and use positive alternatives
- Working with parents as partners when a child has an additional need is essential, what might be the barriers for you as student and how might you overcome them? (Comp: 6.1, 6.4)
- Research autism, create a resource bank that can be used with the team and to support parents and carers. (Comp: 6.2)

VALUES AND BELIEFS

Imagine growing up in a world that has no stories that reflect your life, no images of someone like you and no books or media that portray your life experience in positive ways. Children notice differences because they are curious, and this will happen regardless of whether an adult highlights a difference or not. Favazza and Siperstein (2016) identified disability as a social construct. However, Chih-ing Lim Able-Boone (date) believe in a broader definition of diversity, which includes individual differences in culture race, ethnicity, religion, socioeconomic status, language, gender LBGTQ+, ability and learning styles, arguing that all are critically important for preparing culturally competent learners. Based on the articles of the UNCRC (UNICEF, 1989), there is an explicit commitment to a child's right to equal treatment and voice. Thus, there is a responsibility, to reflect on practice to ensure that children develop a positive sense of belonging through self-identity and group identity:

> Early years settings have an opportunity to prevent prejudices from occurring by ensuring that these children and their families feel welcome and valued. In practice, this means that

settings should ensure that their environments are welcoming and supportive and actively celebrate the value of diversity. Ultimately, supporting children to embrace and celebrate differences between them, their families and others is a crucial part of doing equalities work and fostering inclusive practice.

(The Early Years Coalition, 2021, p. 25)

Books can be a useful way of increasing inclusion awareness in your setting. It is important to share books and stories that include positive representations of our diverse society.

Figure 6.1 shows some examples of books you might share with children. Take time to think about how you will make them part of your everyday practice to ensure you avoid tokenism.

The population of the United Kingdom is diverse, where belonging is continually constructed from within, and society has a responsibility to respond to these continual changes. In your role, you will need to be ready to challenge stereotypical comments. Recognise and accept that you may feel uncomfortable when embarking on these discussions. This should not deter you from taking action.

LONG-TERM IMPACT OF INEQUALITY

In the United Kingdom, there is long standing concern about the educational attainment about certain groups of pupils. The attainment gap cannot be explained by social economic status alone, and may be linked to racism, disability or to cultural and lifestyle differences such as class

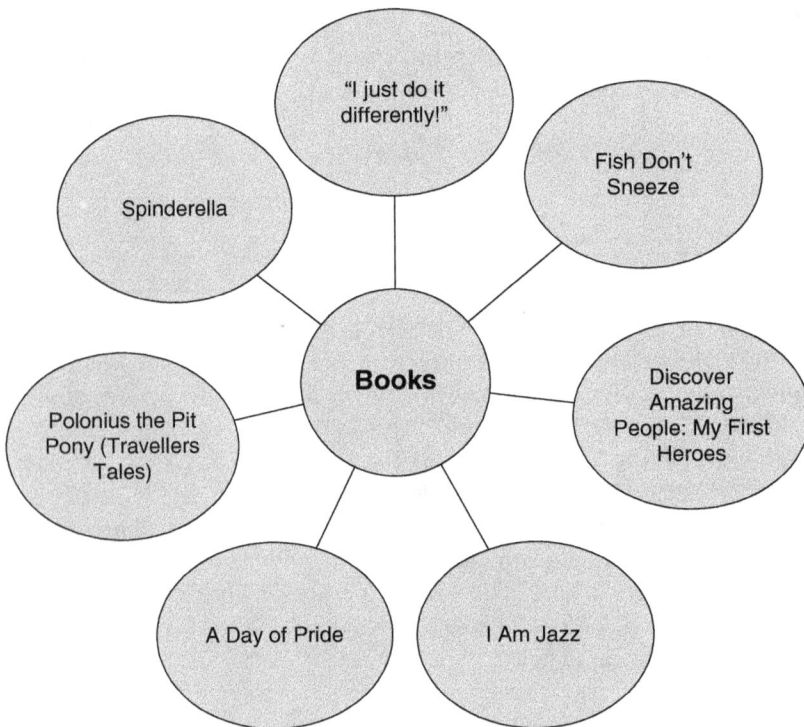

Figure 6.1 Books to share with children

and income. Children start to learn about the world from about the age of two; they begin to ascribe attitudes to people with differences, and from about three years of age, they learn conscious and unconscious prejudices that are prevalent in society (Quintana, 2010). You can address this deficit. Research shows that, 'Less advantaged children who access a high quality, early education programme, achieve better outcomes and enter formal schooling with enhanced school readiness' (Bertram and Pascal, 2016, p. 19).

REFLECTION

- Research the attainment statistics for:
  Gypsy/Roma traveller pupils
  Black pupils
  Chinese pupils
  White working-class boys (see Bertram and Pascal, 2016).
- How will these statistics inform your pedagogy?

As a graduate practitioner, you are encouraged to be reflective and reflexive. You will use theory to examine and analyse your practice and develop your further understanding of inclusive practice. In the act of reflexivity, it is important to be aware of potential, personal biases or shortcomings to explore why and how you know, what you know (Musgrave, 2019) and what has influenced your constructs of people who are different to you. Through the act of reflexivity, you will come to understand something about yourself as a professional. Our understanding of the world is socially constructed (Berger and Luckman, 1966), that is, it exists not in objective reality but because of our interactions with society and environment, for example:

- *we see people with different skin colours, and other physical features and create the social construct of race.*
- *men and women act differently because society has dictated their roles to them. They have learned how they should behave and what they should sound or look like.*

It follows then that our individual world may differ from the children and families we work with. Social constructions can lead to unconscious bias; we need to examine our own values, beliefs and prejudices for unconscious bias, as this may affect how we work with children and families. Noticing differences and similarities in the world is important for children's learning. Engage children in conversations about difference and similarities between people, places and things. Be open to their questions and observations.

REFLECTION

As an early childhood graduate practitioner, you must take care not to make assumptions about children and families, and ensure that you see each child and their circumstances as unique.

(Continued)

(Continued)

- Reflect on your own upbringing and the community in which you live, how might this affect the way you view children and families that have different lives to you?
- Audit your setting for images and resources that develop understanding, and challenge stereotypical, social constructions of the protected characteristics.
- Source resources and books that avoid stereotypical depictions of people.

(Evidence: Competencies: 6.1 and 6.4)

EVIDENCING COMPETENCY 6

Inclusive practice will be evidenced throughout your portfolio. Figure 6.2 identifies some examples of where inclusive practice may be evidenced in other competencies.

CHAPTER SUMMARY

This chapter began by acknowledging the diverse society in which we live and work, recognising that certain groups of people, perceived as 'different' are marginalised. We identified aspects of practice in which, you, as an early childhood graduate practitioner can create a positive approach to inclusion and have a long-term impact on society.

Given the longstanding concerns over the attainment gap of marginalised groups, as early childhood specialists, you will contribute to a child's primary socialisation, how they learn their understanding of their own and other's role and place in society. Your role as a graduate practitioner is to break down barriers to participation and belonging. Resources in the setting have two supporting purposes, providing a window into the lives of others and a reflection of the child in their surroundings (Ellis, 2015; Style, 1988) Children need to be exposed to representations of human differences to help them understand and relate positively to others. The resources serve as a window into our world's diversity.

REFLECTION

- What will you take away from these conversations to use in your own practice?
- How will you continue your professional development in relation to inclusive practice?
- What is representation, and how does it impact you personally in the environment?
- Why are relationships, and getting to know the children and families important to inclusion?

Competency 1:

1.1 demonstrates how you listen to, and work in collaboration with young children individually and in groups

1.2 observe, support and extend young children's participation in their learning through following their needs and interests

1.3 support children to respect others by providing opportunities for their participation and decision-making

Competency 2:

2.2, Demonstrate and apply knowledge of the factors that promote and impede holistic development

Competency 3:

3.1 demonstrate the application of knowledge about health and well-being and safety.

3.3 know and demonstrate how to complete a risk assessment and apply in Practice.

3.4 Ng et al. demonstrate how to complete a risk assessment and apply it to Practice

3.6 have relevant knowledge to support and manage children with ongoing health conditions

Competency 4:

4.1 know and understand the relevant curriculum frameworks and apply them to Practice

4.6 demonstrate knowledge and skill in listening and communicating including situations where: English is an additional language, a child has special educational needs and disabilities

Competency 7:

7.3 apply knowledge to Practice about the diversity of family life and Society

7.4 demonstrate skills in communicating and working in partnership with families

Competency 8:

8.1 evidenced knowledge about the importance of creating successful, respectful professional relationships with colleagues under the professionals in and outside of the setting

8.2 apply collaborative skills in Practice including effective listening and working as a member of a team and in a multi professional context

Competency 9:

9.1 Demonstrate self-awareness and knowledge of anti discriminatory Practice, promoting social justice and the importance of valuing difference

9.2 evidence skills enabling the voice of young children to be heard

9.3 evidence advanced skills in utilising reflective Practice alongside research to enhance your CPD

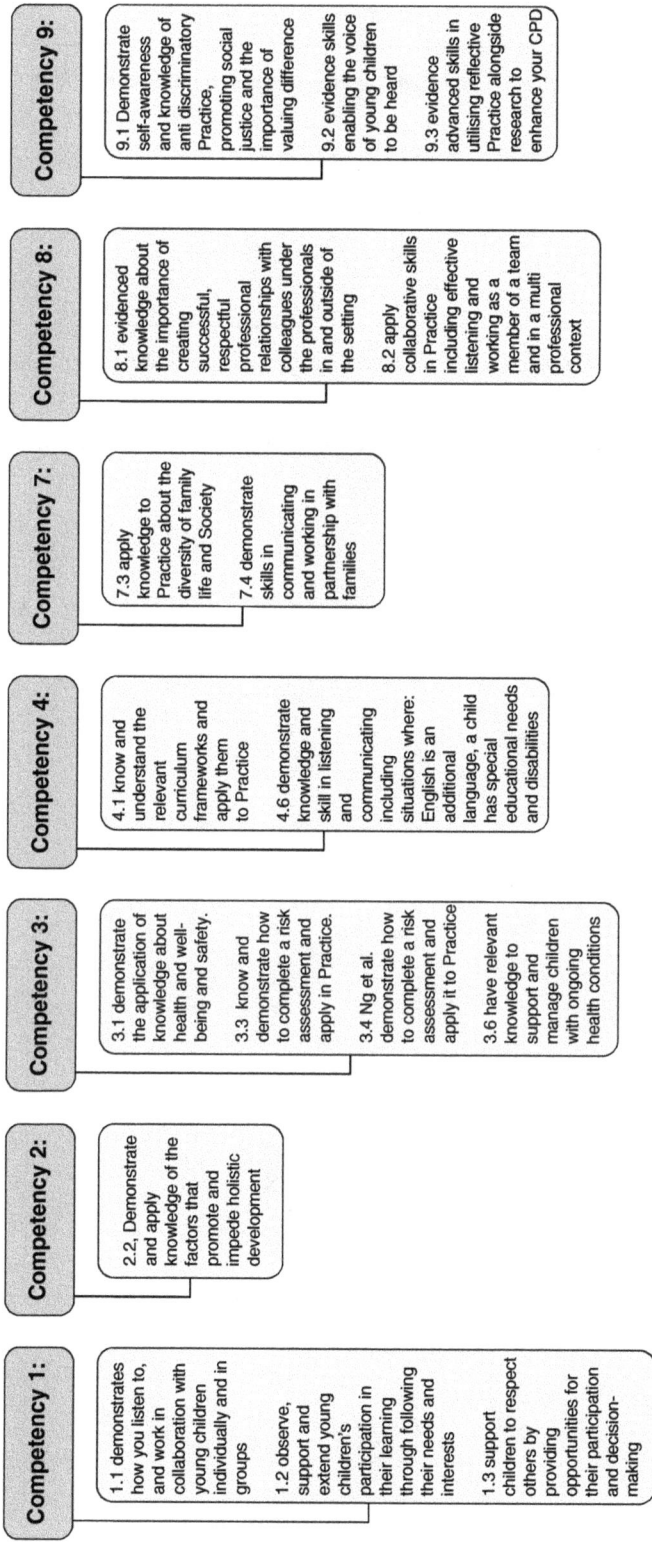

Figure 6.2 Inclusive practice in other competencies

FURTHER READING

Bradbury, A. and Swailes, R. (2022) *Early Childhood Theories Today.* Aaron Bradbury & Ruth Swailes (eds). London: Learning Matters.

Prowle, A. and Hodgkins, A. (2020) *Making a Difference with Children and Families: Re-Imagining the Role of the Practitioner.* London: Bloomsbury Publishing Plc.

WEBSITES

Best children's books that celebrate difference. https://www.penguin.co.uk/articles/childrens-article/childrens-books-that-celebrate-differences-and-diversity

Eight Ways to Show Young Children that Diversity is a Strength – Brookes Blog (brookespublishing.com)

7

PARTNERSHIP WITH PARENTS AND CAREGIVERS

Philippa Thompson

By the end of this chapter, you will be able to:

- Recognise how the values and beliefs of early childhood settings and professionals can significantly influence the styles of partnership working with parents and caregivers.
- Acknowledge the differing policies that have influenced the way early childhood settings and practitioners work with parents and caregivers.
- Recognise how the positioning of parents in society has an influence on how their relationships develop with settings and practitioners.
- Consider how you can recognise and develop your own unconscious bias to develop truly collaborative relationships with parents and caregivers.
- Identify potential sources of evidence in meeting Competency 7: Partnership with Parents.

KEY TERMS AND DEFINITIONS INCLUDED IN THIS CHAPTER

Marginalisation	In this context **marginalisation** is used to describe how processes in early childhood education and care can be designed to exclude some parents from partnership with the setting.
Neoliberalism	**Neoliberalism** is a political ideology that puts the economy at the forefront of early childhood education and care. This involves marketisation of services, measurement of standards by testing and comparison of individuals and settings.
Unconscious bias	**Unconscious bias** describes attitudes and beliefs that are held subconsciously but affect how practitioners and settings might behave towards due to the ways that they perceive them.

INTRODUCTION

Competency 7 sets out the key elements of working in partnership with all adults (with or without parent responsibility) that are involved in supporting the whole family when working in health based, education or social care.

COMPETENCY 7: PARTNERSHIP WITH PARENTS AND CAREGIVERS

7.1 Evidence understanding of the importance of partnership with parents and/or caregivers in their role as infants and young children's first educators.

7.2 Demonstrate in practice the co-construction of learning in respectful partnership with parents and/or caregivers.

7.3 Apply knowledge to practice, about the diversity of family life and society.

7.4 Demonstrate skills in communicating and working in partnership with families.

The theory behind why the concept of partnership with parents and/or caregivers is perceived as important forms the first part of the chapter. The use of the word *partnership* will also be explored considering the political and educational implications of this and whether this is an appropriate word for the work that practitioners do. Benford and Tait (2017) suggest that the relationship between parents/caregivers and early childhood practitioners is essential to the well-being of the child. However, this relationship involves a complexity of critical thinking and reflection to balance policy and practice without enabling the marginalisation of some parents.

This chapter begins by asking what is meant by partnership with parents and/or caregivers and continues by providing an overview of government policy in England over the past 25 years. This policy is explored in the next part of the chapter to consider how policy plays a part in influencing practice as six categories are considered for reflection. The next consideration are the differing perspectives of all those involved. The child, the parents and/or caregivers, students and practitioners and other professionals are all discussed. Finally, a case study and summary support the consideration of practice alongside research and policy for completion of this competency.

WHAT IS PARTNERSHIP WITH PARENTS AND/OR CAREGIVERS?

Parents are positioned in many ways by education and society. One of these positions acknowledges globally that parents/and or caregivers are their child's first educator (Sinaga, Siburian and Siburian, 2020; Dalzell, Watson and Massey, 2009). By the very inference that parents and/or caregivers are the first educator, there could be a suggestion that once their child has started in an educational establishment the parental role in education comes to an end. For this reason, it is interesting to consider language use across research and policy. Whalley et al. (2017) use the term 'co-educator' which suggests an ongoing relationship with families. More recently the term 'co-production', taken from public policy, has become more popular using the idea of active citizenship (Ramsden, 2010). Language is constantly changing, but it is important that those working with young children and families continue to reflect on this and challenge their own perspectives.

In early childhood, there is a strong culture of working in partnership with parents globally. However, as can be seen above from the range of definitions used, this partnership can take many different forms. It is important that these are analysed to consider what might be best practice alongside a consideration of our own unconscious bias. For some, there could be a fear of parents, and that by keeping them at 'arm's length', that is, using power relationships to hide behind, such as the language of the curriculum, allowing parents only to the classroom door or collecting their children in the playground and only meeting to talk for 10 minutes at a parents evening. Is this practice familiar to you? Many practitioners feel threatened professionally by parents and, therefore, it is easier to create a boundary of the practitioner being the professional with all the knowledge, and the caregiver as parenting at home only and who is there to support the practitioner in their role as educator.

Another perspective provides a recognition that developing quality relationships with parents and caregivers can make the practitioner role more enjoyable and can evolve into a co-production of curriculum and learning, where engagement benefits the child and the others around them. Practice might involve parents and caregivers being part of the morning routine by entering the space and engaging in activities with their children. Practitioners can be there to support and have conversations about any difficulties currently going on or indeed successes or exciting events from the night before! When children are struggling to settle, the practitioner will probably understand why, due to having developed a strong relationship and the ability to support the parent/caregiver to leave when it works for everyone.

It is important for us to understand why these different positions evolve as both styles would consider they are using their approach in the best interests of the child. The place to start is policy as this has had a significant impact on practice and not always in the most positive ways.

AN OVERVIEW OF POLICY

Policy is complex in ECEC as governance is spread across a range of government departments, including education, health, work and pensions (Hasan, 2007). Current research literature suggests that these policy contexts can influence familial experiences and quality of life (Bollinger et al., 2006; Cohen et al., 2004). The early childhood years are a crucial time when parents and/or caregivers may leave the home environment during the day or night and return to work. They may enlist the support of their wider community and make decisions for their child in leaving them to be cared for outside the home. This provides a huge responsibility for those working in early childhood to ensure that the needs of all children and their families are met.

It could be argued that have not fully been supported by Government policy which despite many references to parents, has not provided a streamlined initiative to working with and supporting parents across the United Kingdom. There appears to be a clash of ideologies where the government focuses on the economy and getting parents back to work, while at the same time having an expectation that parents should be working closely with practitioners in a collaborative way. The following Table 7.1 outlines the key areas of policy over the past 25

Table 7.1   Key policy milestones

Date	Policy	Implications
2004	Choice for Parents, the Best Start for Children (HM Treasury)	A ten-year childcare strategy. The term 'good quality affordable childcare' involved support for parents financially, increase in paid maternity time, hours were increased to 15 hours per week for free nursery education.
2006	Childcare Act	Local authorities were deemed responsible for securing adequate provision of childcare for working parents. The emphasis is again on childcare.
2010	Free Nursery education for two-year-olds introduced	This created a clash of emphasis on quantity versus quality. The idea of affordable childcare against the qualifications of the workforce providing more than simply childcare.
2011	Early Intervention: The Next Steps – Allen Report	There was a positioning of parents as hard to reach and vulnerable. Positive interventions such as a continuation of the family nurse partnership were highlighted and a proposal that the healthy start initiative and the EYFS should be more streamlined.
2013	More Affordable Childcare	This included a new tax-free childcare scheme for working families
2013	More great childcare: Raising quality and giving parents more choice	Introduction of early years teacher status and early years educator qualifications.
2015	'Building Great Britons', published by the All-Party Parliamentary Group for Conception to Age 2 – The First 1,001 Days	This highlights a central role for children's centres, antenatal and perinatal support and early intervention.
2018	Evidence-based Early Years Intervention. The Science and Technology Select Committee	Makes the link with adverse childhood experiences and later life usage of health and social care services.
2019	Tackling disadvantage in the Early Years. The Education Select Committee	This cross-party report criticises government policy on early years. Recommendations are balanced on the premise that to reduce disadvantage children need quality early years provision and a quality home environment.
2019	First 1000 Days of Life. The Health and Social Care Select Committee.	Highlights the role of the family, the number of health visitor visits and continuity of care past 1,000 days.
2020	Ipsos, M. O. R. I. (2020). State of the nation: Understanding public attitudes to the early years.	Report by the Royal Foundation with a key focus on positive encouragement of the role of parents with under-fives.
2021	The Best Start for Life: A Vision for the 1,001 Critical Days. The Early Years Healthy Development Review Report. HM Government.	Formed part of the early year's healthy development review. Six areas for action were outlined to support the improvement of all babies in England.

years where the ethos seems to waver between providing support for parents but then suggesting that parents also need to be supporters (Duffy and Pugh, 2013).

As is evident in Table 7.1, there is a strong focus on early childhood and parents/families from conception. Since 1997, governments have acknowledged that early childhood is a significant part of life in terms of learning, development and health. Each report identifies that the role of the family is significant, that qualified professionals across a range of disciplines make a difference and that early intervention can make an important difference to children's lives as they become older. However, the stumbling block appears to be finance and a clear strategy on how to develop such services. The confusion between the use of the word childcare that should be affordable and the quality of provision and home support does not seem to have moved further. Instead, small changes and proposals such as reducing ratios seem to contradict the evidence in the above reports and focus on affordable rather than quality. As Yerkes and Javornik (2019, p. 537) identify, '*Availability, accessibility and affordability provide the foundation for childcare capabilities; quality only becomes an issue once childcare is available and accessible, and is often a reflection of affordability*'. The follow-on effect is that a less-qualified workforce can keep costs down particularly where childcare is marketised and seen as profit making, e.g., private day nurseries. Parents and caregivers paying for a service and seen as consumers may be less willing or have less time available to developing a quality home environment alongside the setting. A less qualified workforce may not have access to the necessary experience, research and knowledge to support parents and/or caregivers in a meaningful way. This is not to say that this does not exist but that it is less likely to be consistent for families and children without clear policy, strategy and a highly qualified workforce.

HOW DOES POLICY INFLUENCE OUR OWN PERCEPTION OF PARENTS?

Through analysis of the current research and policy literature on parents, there are potentially six ways in which parents and caregivers could be positioned by policy in early childhood. Depending on the practitioner and setting viewpoint, this can have an impact on how parents and caregivers are enabled to co-collaborate. The six positions are briefly defined below:

- as generators of school/setting improvement
- as first educator with the power to improve outcomes for children
- as workforce
- as achievers of social and economic success
- as empowered with choice: a consumerist voice
- as marginalised by parenting styles and accessibility.

It is important to challenge your own unconscious bias about the roles of parents to consider what a true partnership looks like. By considering the six suggestions above, this enables you to develop your own thinking and critical reflection.

This section of the chapter has analysed a selection of the current relevant policy and research in relation to the experiences of parents and caregivers. It has considered how policy impacts on practice in early childhood and how, when working with young children, we must have an awareness of how these impact on our own behaviours and the behaviours of the setting. Having an awareness that our own personal and professional backgrounds have an influence on how we build relationships with parents is important to consider. The chapter will now move on to analyse the perspectives of all those involved in the development of positive relationships with parents and caregivers. This aims to support those completing their early childhood graduate practitioner competencies and consider the contribution of parents and caregivers.

OTHER PERSPECTIVES

When working with parents and caregivers, policy and research need to pay strong attention to those involved in practice and consider their perspectives. This part of the chapter will pose some suggestions to encourage you to reflect about your own practice while considering the perspective of the child, those of parents and caregivers, students and practitioners and other professionals. The following themes aim to support readers to look through a different lens. It is always difficult to understand the lives of others when it is not a lived experience but critical reflection and empathy are valuable tools to begin to further inclusivity of children and their families.

PERSPECTIVE OF THE CHILD

The earliest years of a child's life can determine whether they will thrive, learn and develop in life. Their development is dependent on those adults that provide their care, and this could be a wider network than simply those with parental responsibility. The United Nations Convention of the Rights of the Child (UNCRC) (1989) outlines the need for children's voices to be heard and that part of a practitioner role is to create child agency. This suggestion demonstrates the need for parental voice to be heard as well as those of the caregivers as they will understand their own child's needs. They can also provide a voice for those who are too young to have their own.

Understanding a child's socio-economic standing such as family income, living circumstances, parental styles and any stresses that may be influencing the child are important factors in considering how the voice of the child can be heard. Good practitioners will also be open to understanding issues surrounding race and racism and have policies in place to support both children and parents. Talking and building relationships with those that are closest to the child are important in providing that all important agency. It is not acceptable to make assumptions about a child without understanding their individual lifestyles and the adults that are important to them.

REFLECTION

- How would you ensure you have time to talk to parents away from their children?
- Do you remember to think about whether your conversation with parents is one that you should be having with the child present?
- How do you ensure that the child's voice is heard regardless of the age of the child? What strategies can you think of?

PARENTS AND CAREGIVERS

This chapter encourages you to think about your relationships with parents and caregivers, and highlights how we need to consider our own unconscious bias. Hamilton (2021, p. 1) states that 'Marginalisation can be understood as both a process, and a condition, that prevents individuals or groups from full participation in social, economic and political life.' This quotation provides a starting point for meaningful reflection. Thinking about conversations and assumptions, it is important to put yourself in the place of the parent. If you are labelling them as 'hard to reach', for example, have you in fact considered whether those parents and caregivers feel marginalised by your behaviour or approach? Perhaps they feel marginalised by the way policy is enacted in your setting? Have these discussions taken place to find out or has blame been apportioned before this?

There is potential in the concept of co-production rather than simply 'partnership' which is defined in current research to have the impact of enabling inclusive partnerships with parents of all children. Understanding the lived experience of parents and caregivers develops strong and meaningful relationships rather than those that could be considered as tokenistic.

REFLECTION

- How would you ensure that you reflect on your own unconscious bias to consider relationships and working practices with parents and caregivers?
- Reflect on practice that you have already observed in practice. Would you describe it as partnership, co-production or marginalisation?

STUDENTS AND PRACTITIONERS

This section does not suggest that the role of students and practitioners is an easy one. For students, it can be difficult to be seen as part of the working team if you are in for placement. This is a difficult base from which to build relationships but not impossible. It can also be seen as an opportunity to have conversations and find out more about the family and in turn build trusting relationships. Both students and practitioners have wide ranging roles when working with young children and often consider that the child is at the heart of their priorities rather than the parent or caregiver. During the global pandemic early childhood practitioners were identified as key workers (Department for Education (DfE), 2020). While the role at this time was recognised as an asset to society, it has not been rewarded in terms of career structures and salaries. Qualifications vary and as a graduate you could be expected to lead in areas such as parent partnerships. It is important to continue to reflect and read while working towards this qualification to develop your own beliefs and ideas based in research to support your work. Parental cultures may differ widely, but how do you ensure that everyone feels welcome and equally valued? Talking is a starting place even if some of those conversations are uncomfortable and can lead to diversity being celebrated and supported.

OTHER PROFESSIONALS

Many different professionals work with parents and caregivers, and it is important to remember that while positive to receive support, this can also be confusing and intimidating for families, when professionals may view it as supportive. Professionals can position themselves as the expert on the child and the parent or caregiver has no choice but to adopt a passive role. This can happen across all professions such as social work, health practitioners and in education and equally there can be some excellent practice. As a key worker for the family in early childhood, is there a role for practitioners to understand how many professionals are involved with a family and how these relationships differ? Working with parents and caregivers to encourage agency and a desire to be a collaborative partner involves stepping back from the role of expert and handing over this role to those who know their child best. This role can fluctuate as sometimes families may be looking for advice and sometimes professionals will be looking for collaboration. Working together is not easy but provides many benefits and can lead to quality collaboration for everyone concerned.

The following case study illustrates how Asma used an example from practice to meet Competency 7.

CASE STUDY 1

During her level 5 placement, Asma became really interested in the family learning groups being held in the children's centre where she was working. She asked if she could attend the sessions once a week to see how parents/caregivers and practitioners were working together to build relationships and support their children's learning and development. This was a competency that Asma had found previously difficult to observe at level 4 in a primary school as students had been discouraged from engaging with parents. After attending for a couple of weeks, Asma realised that she would be able to collect evidence across the whole of Competency 7 in this way as her own relationships with parents began to develop.

The sessions were held in a community room in the children's centre where refreshments were available for all of those who were attending. The practitioner running the sessions had already built a strong relationship with the parents and caregivers and had asked about what was culturally appropriate to provide. As the sessions continued, parents and caregivers began to bring their own food to share with the group and Asma noticed how this socially developed a bond between the group and the practitioners. As a bilingual student Asma was also able to see how her own skill to support some of the mothers who were still learning English would also provide a thoughtful reflection for her portfolio (7.2, 7.3 and 7.4).

The sessions guided by the practitioner involved understanding children's learning at home and how this could be shared with practitioners to support relationships, their own child's development and how practitioners could share the language of the EYFS so that parents and caregivers could see the

(Continued)

(Continued)

difference they were making. The practitioner had been inspired by attending a course at Pen Green Centre in Corby, Northamptonshire, and had developed her own sessions from this. Each week the session would focus on involvement, well-being, play and schematic behaviour. Parents and caregivers would then use their mobile phones to take photos of their children at home, with family and outdoors when they felt they were deeply involved, were showing a particular characteristic of well-being (Laevers, 2000) or demonstrating a particular schema (Nutbrown and Atherton, 2013). Parents and caregivers would bring the photos to the next session and print a selection to talk about and add to their 'portfolio' about their child or children. The practitioner would then support this using the children's centre record keeping system to show how what was happening at home supported their children's development and learning. Asma was able to use her knowledge from her modules at university to support the families' understanding while also supporting practitioners to have a deeper cultural understanding of home environments.

COMMENTARY ON CASE STUDY 1

To develop her portfolio, Asma wrote a reflective account of her experience using current literature from a recent module to support 7.1 *Evidence understanding of the importance of partnership with parents and/or caregivers in their role as infants and young children's first educators.* She also wrote a reflective account to support 7.2 *Demonstrate in practice the co-construction of learning in respectful partnership with parents and/or caregivers* where she described how the course was set up to be welcoming, respectful and developed co construction through sharing home and setting experiences. When *applying knowledge to practice, about the diversity of family life and society* (7.3) Asma asked permission from one family to share one page of their portfolio which shared evidence of home, how that linked to the EYFS (DfE, 2021a) and supported practitioners' cultural awareness (challenging unconscious bias). Asma wrote some short notes and included these. Finally, the practitioner signed a witness statement for Asma about how she had worked with parents and caregivers and led two of the sessions using her bilingual skills. This was evidence for 7.4, *Demonstrate skills in communicating and working in partnership with families.*

REFLECTION

1. How will you ensure that you can engage with parents and caregivers during at least one of your placements? You may need to be proactive for this to happen.
2. What are the theoretical links to your answer?

(Continued)

(Continued)

3. What are the implications for your practice, and how are you going to improve or change your practice?
4. How are you going to continue your professional development in relation to partnership with parents and caregivers?

COMMENT

How are you going to ensure that your relationships with parents and caregivers are about co-construction rather than built on assumption and power?

CHAPTER SUMMARY

This chapter highlights the importance of rethinking traditional methods of working with parents and the term 'partnership'. As part of your graduate practitioner competencies, you will need to evidence your understanding of why it is important to work alongside parents and caregivers and why this relationship is so valuable. The chapter supports your understanding of the positioning of parents particularly in England through policy and practitioner perception and how you can use this knowledge to reflect on your own beliefs and practice. Six perspectives are explored through a collation of the literature and policy and explored for you to continue your own reflection. While it is important to develop our own perspectives, the chapter also explores the perspectives of others involved as when true collaboration occurs then all needs must be considered. The demonstration of good practice in terms of co-collaboration with parents and/or caregivers is explored through reflective questions to support your understanding of which elements of your practice could be used as evidence. The case study outlines one student's approach to being proactive in organising placement opportunities when working with parents and caregivers. As suggested in the chapter, as a student, it can be difficult to build parent and family relationships. However, there are ways in which you may be able to make this happen by discussing it with your setting. Understanding the diversity of family life and wider society is a crucial part of working in a way that is inclusive of everyone. Once you begin to develop this understanding, you will become more confident at being able to demonstrate your own ways of communicating and working in partnership with families.

Before working in partnership with parents and caregivers it is important to decide the following:

- What is your definition of partnership and why?
- How will you ensure that when working with parents and/or caregivers that you understand your own unconscious bias and that of others?
- Why do you think it is important to work with parents and/or caregivers?

FURTHER READING

Thompson, P. and Simmons, H. (2023) *Partnership with parents in early childhood today.* London. Learning Matters.

8

COLLABORATING WITH OTHERS

Leanne Gray and *Michelle Wisbey*

By the end of this chapter, you will be able to:

- Understand the significance of sharing information between settings, families and other stakeholders.
- Build a community around the child.
- Understand the importance of giving children a voice.
- Collaborate with children, families, colleagues and other stakeholders.
- Understand the barriers to working with others and have strategies to address these.

KEY TERMS AND DEFINITIONS INCLUDED IN THIS CHAPTER

Community	The community includes all those involved in the child's life. For example, parents, nursery practitioners, health visitor, educational psychologist.
Collaboration	Working with others to achieve a goal or complete a task.
Professional relationships	The relationship between individuals or groups of people in a work environment, including relationships with colleagues, your mentor, parents of children at the setting and with other professionals.
Communities of practice	A group of people who share a common concern for something and then improve practice by working together (Lave and Wenger, 1991).

INTRODUCTION

The three case studies in this chapter will demonstrate how practitioners embed collaborating with others in their settings. Case Study 1 explores how the sharing of knowledge through communities of practice can lead to positive solutions to problems in the setting which impact both the children and the parents as well as the practitioners. Case Study 2 illustrates the importance of listening to young children and how, by giving children a voice, a potentially harmful incident can be turned around to a positive experience for the child. The final case study considers the impact of the community around the child, and how communication can support a child's transition into a setting. Through these case studies you will learn the importance of collaborating and listening to others. This will support you in achieving the early childhood graduate practitioner competency (ECGPC) in three ways. Firstly, you will understand the importance of building successful relationships with children, parents, colleagues and other professionals. Secondly, you will learn the importance of effective communication and team working and finally, you will understand some of the barriers to successful collaboration, and how to overcome these.

This chapter will explore Competency 8 which explores collaboration with others. Underpinning daily life in an early childhood setting is the importance of creating successful, respectful and professional relationships with colleagues and other professionals both within and outside the setting. Working as a member of a team and in multi-professional contexts can result in challenges and barriers. However, collaborative working in practice, including effective listening, can reduce the impact of these challenges and barriers. In this chapter, we consider how ECGPC students can develop their understanding of collaborating with others in both a theoretical and practical context.

The chapter presents three examples from practice that help you to see how this competency relates to everyday practice in Early Years (EY) settings. The first two case studies are from Michelle Wisbey. Case Study 1 demonstrates how practitioners can develop collaborative conversations through communities of practice and Case Study 2 demonstrates the importance of practitioners giving children a voice. The third case study is from Leanne Gray and demonstrates how practitioners can make collaborative links between the communities around the child. Through exploring these case studies, we outline how you can understand and evidence your work towards the competencies.

Case Study 1 illustrates an example of how collaboration between stakeholders, including the ECGPC student in the nursery environment, can bring about positive change. It demonstrates an understanding of how the barriers to working with others can be overcome and how to address these in practice.

COMPETENCY 8: COLLABORATING WITH OTHERS

8.1 Evidence knowledge about the importance of creating successful, respectful professional relationships with colleagues and other professionals in and outside the setting.

8.2 Apply collaborative skills in practice, including effective listening and working as a member of a team and in multi-professional contexts.

8.3 Demonstrate an understanding of the barriers to working with other and how to address these in practice.

SHARING KNOWLEDGE THROUGH COMMUNITIES OF PRACTICE

CASE STUDY 1 – COLLABORATIVE CONVERSATIONS THROUGH COMMUNITIES OF PRACTICE

During COVID the parents had not been allowed in the Nursery setting. Once the Government had lifted restrictions, this element of the day needed to be revisited on request from the parents, who wanted to be allowed back into the setting at drop-off and pick-up times, as they had done pre-COVID. The practitioner team were keen to keep this restriction in place, as they felt children settled more quickly on arrival, and as a result, the transition to the morning routine was quicker, with less interruptions. It was suggested that someone could spend some time speaking with parents and the children and gather their views. This was an ideal opportunity for the ECGPC student.

After views had been gathered, and to help find a resolution, the practitioner team proposed a forum-type evening with the parents. This evening was held, and has become a bi-monthly event, now called 'collaborative conversation evening' (Wisbey, 2021). The collaborative conversation gives opportunity for the voice of parents and the staff team to be heard. Ideas are also shared with the children, and their views sort, during their Nursery day.

The outcome of the collaboration between communities of practice has meant that a solution was found that has enhanced partnership with parents and their involvement in the setting, with opportunity sought to involve the ECGPC student. Three different procedures were put into place:

1. *Parents are asked to drop-off at the door in the mornings but are invited into the setting when they pick their children up.*
2. *Parents (one at a time) can request to spend some time in the Nursery helping with learning activities or other parts of the daily routine. If this is being organised, their child sends the parent an invitation to join them in their Nursery.*
3. *Reflective conversation after the parent's time in the Nursery to discuss their child's Nursery community and experiences of both parent and child, developing 'in reality' connectiveness and involvement.*

COMMENTARY ON CASE STUDY 1

This case study evidences how collaboration within communities of practice in the nursery created new opportunities for successful, respectful partnership with parents, the parent's partnership with the nursery and empowerment of the child. For the practitioner and for the ECGPC student who gathered the views and were part of the collaborative conversation, it developed a firm partnership between parent, child and nursery. It brought about educational change and developed understanding and knowledge of the involved community cultures.

You would also consider here how you would give children a voice as part of the collaboration. Giving children a voice of their own, as advocated by the UNCRC (1989) rather than through the adult, has been a growing sentiment to support children's participation in their own lives (Kanyal, 2014). By including the children and listening to them, we can better understand their local knowledge, their attention to detail and their visual and verbal communication skills. It is possible to use inclusive child friendly methods to support the child's voice, such as the use of photographic media, story tours, observation and role playing and idea bouncing (Wisbey, 2021). Giving the children these opportunities enable the ECGPC student to construct their knowledge and observe children empowered in constructing their knowledge.

REFLECTION

Identify some areas where collaboration of communities of practice could enhance the practice in the early years setting.

Can you think of anything else that could be done to strengthen the collaboration between the community of the nursery?

THE IMPORTANCE OF LISTENING TO YOUNG CHILDREN

Case Study 2 illustrates how Michelle put her collaborative skills into practice and effectively listened to a child who, in turn, was able to communicate an incident with his parents. As you read the case study, consider how Michelle's approach helped to give the child agency.

CASE STUDY 2: GIVING CHILDREN A VOICE

The children in the nursery were carrying out normal nursery activities. One of these activities, as part of caring for their environment, was to feed and clean out the chickens. When the children were ready to leave, the chicken run one of the children bent down to speak to a chicken and ask her nicely to move out of the way. The hen took offence to this and promptly pecked him on the lip, resulting in lots of blood and many tears.

Normally, the member of staff present would complete the accident form and then give it to the parent/carer when they arrive to pick up their child. But this time, to try and settle the child and take his mind off the incident, the child was asked to tell the story of what happened, and the member of staff wrote the story down word for word. The child then shared their own name, and other details that needed to go on the form. This collaboration gave the

(Continued)

(Continued)

child a voice, empowering him to take ownership of what happened. He was informed and understood the situation. And, at the very least it settled him down and took his mind off the situation. The power of this action did not stop there. At pick-up time, the child carried the accident book to his parent and retold the story and explained why she needed to sign it. The parent then reported back that the story was retold at home.

COMMENTARY ON CASE STUDY 2

This case study illustrates an example of giving children a voice. The context is an everyday occurrence in early years settings: accidents and incidents. These incidents are part of the rich tapestry of the day and should not be viewed as a negative element. The case study demonstrates how an incident can be turned around.

This simple example case study of how collaboration with one of the most important stakeholders in the nursery, the child, created so many developmental opportunities for not only the child but also for the practitioner and for the ECGPC student who supported the child at pick-up time, and from this developed a firm partnership between child, parent and nursery.

Giving children a voice of their own, as advocated by the UNCRC (1989) rather than through an adult, has been a popular sentiment used to support children's participation (Kanyal, 2014), in their learning journey. Collaboration with children is argued by some to be challenging, but Clark (2004) suggests that it is 'a methodology which plays to young children's strengths rather than weaknesses – their local knowledge, their attention to detail and visual as well as verbal communication skills' (p. 153). Through collaboration, it is possible to develop methods that met the needs of both the culture and the child. Such a balanced and inclusive approach resonates with Montessori, respecting each child as an independent individual with understanding of themselves, their environment, their needs and their interests. Yet allowing children to participate fully can pose a problem, particularly when you include the collaboration between the two other elements of the early years setting: the adult and the environment. Morrow and Richards (1996) contend that one of the biggest ethical challenges in working with children in an early years setting is the disparities in power and status between stakeholders, particularly when you consider children are normally reliant on adults and adults view this reliance as part of the natural order (Qvortrup, 1994). When carrying out tasks and observations for the ECGPC, collaboration will create some form of equality (Freeman and Mathison, 2009).

Seeing the child as a competent voice of their own experience and understanding their family culture is vital and must be appropriate to the child's age and level of understanding, thus enabling the child to participate fully. As an ECGPC student you will learn more about the needs of the children by adopting a role that aligns more to observing the participation and behaviour of the children (Freeman and Mathison, 2009). The construction of the knowledge gained through collaboration with the child will inform learning, social and cultural experiences. Collaboration ensures opportunity for the children to tell alternative narrative in their own way and in response to their positionality in their community (Moss, 2019).

REFLECTION

What further activities could be done with the child to support their understanding?

COLLABORATIVE LINKS BETWEEN THE COMMUNITIES AROUND THE CHILD

In Case Study 3, Leanne explains how a collaborative approach with Asma and her parents helped to settle Asma down into the routines of the nursery.

CASE STUDY 3: COLLABORATIVE LINKS BETWEEN THE COMMUNITIES AROUND THE CHILD

Asma is three years old and is joining a pre-school for the first time. She has previously been looked after by her immediate family (Mum and Dad). As her start date approaches, the pre-school manager contacts Asma's parents and explains the transition and settling-in policies and procedures. During the phone call, Asma's mother reveals she is very anxious about Asma starting pre-school and thinks that Asma will cry during the whole session. Asma's mother states that she would like Asma to have some time in pre-school so that she can be more prepared for school. The pre-school manager notes all this information and, as per the policy, arranges a meeting at the setting between Asma's parents, Asma and Asma's keyworker. The information is passed on to Asma's keyworker, Kate. At the meeting, Asma clings to Mum. Kate finds out about Asma's interests and explains the settling in process to Asma's parents. Mum or Dad will be able to attend with Asma for short periods so that Asma can become more comfortable in the pre-school and begin to get to know Kate and the other members of staff with the support of Mum or Dad. Only when Asma is ready, does Mum leave Asma for short periods of time, while waiting in the reception area of the pre-school. Gradually, over several weeks, Asma is confident in the pre-school and Mum and Dad are confident leaving Asma for a whole morning session.

COMMENTARY ON CASE STUDY 3

This case study illustrates the importance of good communication between the family and the setting when a child joins the setting for the first time. Bronfenbrenner's (1979, 1994) theory is particularly relevant during periods of transition in a child's life. This case study involves a child joining a setting for the first time, having previously been at home with their primary caregivers. As the child moves from being a member of a family group to being a member of the setting, it is crucial to ensure good communication between the family and the setting. The communication between the parents and the setting was crucial in ensuring that Asma settled confidently in the setting. Each setting will have specific transition processes which will include communicating to find out the child's interests, how they can be comforted, sleep patterns, diet, etc. As detailed in the case study, this transition can be eased through the role of the key person in the Early Years Foundation Stage (EYFS) (DfE, 2021a) who should take the time to get to know the child and closely support both the child and their family during the settling in process.

Once a child is established and settled in a setting, regular communication between home and setting is essential to support the child's ongoing development. This can be informal conversations at picking up and dropping off time, through online communication tools, through written records about the child's development both at home and in the setting and through more formal meetings between the key person and the parent. It is important that this communication is a two-way process, and that the setting seeks to find out information about the child's development at home.

We consider the collaborative links between the communities around the child through the lens of the **ecological systems theory (as outlined in Chapter 2)** (Bronfenbrenner, 1979, 1994).

Bronfenbrenner's ecological systems theory is particularly relevant to this competency because it highlights the importance of good communication between the home, the setting and anyone else involved in the child's development. This may include the child's immediate family and their extended family as well as outside agencies such as a health visitor, speech and language therapist, social worker or SEN support worker. Good communication between these parties will ensure everyone is working together in the best interests of the child.

Developing collaboration between groups of people who share a concern or a passion for something they do and learn can develop a feeling of connectiveness and involvement and create a feeling of positiveness and energy (Wenger, 1998). BERA/TACTYC (2017) supports the development of learning or practice communities, to support practitioner–learners through supervision and mentoring, as key to professional development for quality practice. Communities of practice are beneficial and enable learners to meet the learning outcomes (Lave and Wenger, 1991) of the ECGPC. Wenger (1998) highlights five critical functions of learning communities, which support ECGPC students in developing skills to overcome the barriers of collaboration:

- Educate by collecting and sharing information related to questions and issues of practice
- Support by organising interactions and collaboration among members
- Cultivate by assisting groups to start and sustain their learning
- Encourage by promoting the work of members through discussion and sharing
- Integrate by encouraging members to use their new knowledge for real change in their own work.

These functions support the development of educational relationships and demonstrate how they co-exist. They provide a shared context for people to communicate and share information, stories and personal experiences in a way that builds understanding and insight about the young children. They also enable dialogue between colleagues to explore new possibilities, solve challenging problems and create new, mutually beneficial opportunities. These functions stimulate learning by serving as a vehicle for communication, mentoring, coaching and self-reflection. They also create opportunity to capture and share existing knowledge about practice by providing a forum to identify solutions to common problems and a process to collect and evaluate best practices. These functions also generate new knowledge to enable ECGPC students to transform their practice for the benefit of children and families. This enables ECGPC students to organise purposeful actions that develop tangible results.

Sharing knowledge through communities of practice also acknowledges that educational relationships are often intercultural and how members of the practice community relate to each other is influenced by the 'socio-historical and political contexts of those engaging' (Pirbhai-Illich and Martin, 2020, p. 57). Indeed, through the ECGPC, a deeper understanding will develop improving your understanding of different contextual and cultural identities (Martin and Griffiths, 2014).

The collaborative nature developed through the ECGPC is done so through a leadership lens. Ideas for change and development are reliant on critically reflection on the student's own knowledge and practice, as well as respecting the voice, practices and funds of knowledge (Moll et al., 1992) of other stakeholders in the community. Opportunity for this knowledge sharing can be developed using collaborative conversations (Wisbey, 2021); thus, the contribution of knowledge and voice that can bring about equitable change (Mac Naughton and Hughes, 2009) is drawn from the community of practice.

REFLECTION

What could be the impact on the child's development if the parents/carers and setting do not share information about the child?

Reflect on the communication practices you have seen in any schools/settings where you have worked. Are they effective? How could they be improved?

CHAPTER SUMMARY

This chapter develops discussion about how collaborating with others underpins successful practice in early years settings. Building a community around the child involving the children, parents, practitioners and other relevant professionals develops connectiveness and involvement, thus creating a feeling of positiveness and energy between those involved (Wenger, 1998).

This chapter has illustrated the importance of collaborating with others. While on placement, ECGPC students should seek out opportunities to develop collaboration skills by observing experienced practitioners and by applying these skills themselves with support from a mentor. By being inclusive, the community of practice (Wenger, 1998) is a safe place for the ECGPC student to belong, to develop and to grow in collaboration with peers and practitioners.

FURTHER READING

Moss, P. (2019) *Alternative Narratives in Early Childhood: An Introduction for Students and Practitioners.* Abingdon: Routledge.

Wenger, E. (1998) *Communities of Practice: Learning, Meaning, and Identity.* Cambridge: Cambridge University Press.

9

PROFESSIONAL DEVELOPMENT

Meredith Rose, Stella Smith and *Matt Northall*

By the end of this chapter, you will be able to:

- Demonstrate self-awareness and knowledge of anti-discriminatory practice.
- Engage in the literature which supports the need for a robust critical knowledge of reflective practice.
- Develop an ongoing dialogue of practice and theoretical concepts to gain graduate knowledge and understandings of the importance of continuing professional development.
- Demonstrate the ability to apply theory to early childhood practice while gathering evidence for your graduate practitioner competencies.

KEY TERMS AND DEFINITIONS INCLUDED IN THIS CHAPTER

Definitions	Explanation
Early childhood or EC, and early years	EC refers to the age group of children from 0 to 7 years. Sometimes this appears as EC or in European terms ECEC (early childhood education and care).
	The term 'early years' is referred to in policy and government documents which is a slightly narrower age range and usually refers to children aged between 0 and 5 years in education and care settings.
Pedagogical beliefs	Each practitioner will have their own pedagogical beliefs which drive their actions and approaches to providing play and learning activities for children. Influences may arise from a mixture of evidence-based practice, theory and philosophy.
Developing graduate practitioner	The journey that a graduate will take when embarking upon a degree with graduate practitioner competencies (GPC).

INTRODUCTION

This chapter will explore Competency 9: Professional development. Professional development is the process of engaging and reflecting upon emerging debates and practices within our ECEC discipline. CPD is not limited to individuals and their actions but also includes communities of practice and can be delivered through a variety of means including online and distance learning.

COMPETENCY 9: PROFESSIONAL DEVELOPMENT

9.1 Demonstrate self-awareness and knowledge of anti-discriminatory practice, promoting social justice and the importance of valuing difference, including gender, ethnicity, religious affiliation and sexual orientation.

9.2 Evidence skills in enabling the voice if young children to be heard.

9.3 Evidence advanced skills in utilising reflective practice alongside research, to enhance your continual professional development in early childhood.

9.4 Draw on research to demonstrate knowledge of leadership and management and its importance and application in democratic and inclusive practice.

9.5 Recognise and evidence the importance of communicating effectively orally and in writing to others.

This chapter presents two examples from practice that help you to see how this competency relates to everyday practice in ECEC settings. The first case study is from Jasmine, a graduate practitioner, and demonstrates how practitioners work alongside other professionals to maximise the impact on quality outcomes for children.

The second is Gavin, an experienced practitioner, and demonstrates the complexities and pressures facing practitioners in the ECEC sector as well as the importance of reflecting and continually improving practice for the benefit of practitioner, children and families.

Through exploring these case studies, we outline how you can understand and evidence your work towards the competencies as you develop as an ECEC graduate practitioner.

CURRENT PRACTICE AS AN EARLY CHILDHOOD GRADUATE PRACTITIONER

There are many aspects of professional development to think of, including how our own values and practices give way to develop a self-awareness and to gain further knowledge of anti-discriminatory practice, promoting social justice and the importance of valuing difference. Professional development provides a place for further learning of inclusive practices. They form part of our day-to-day roles. It comes with a commitment of valuing and respecting the diversity of an individual (Bradbury, 2022). As stated in the Birth to 5 Matters Guidance, 'settings have a

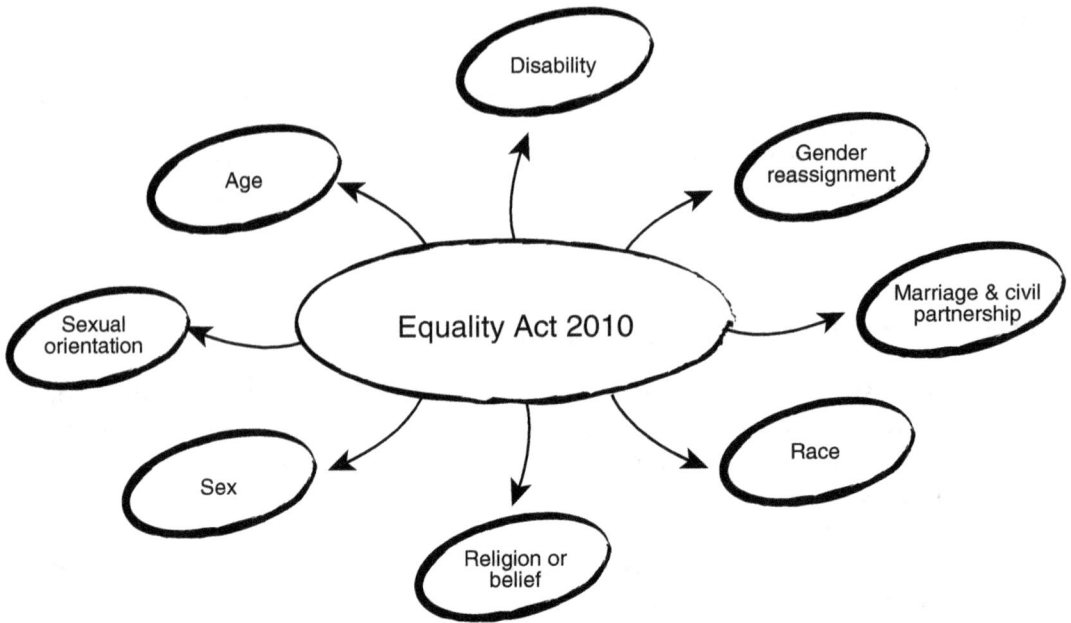

Figure 9.1 Equality act 2010 – Characteristics (Bradbury and Swailes, 2022)

vital role to play in explicitly addressing all forms of discrimination and prejudices' (2021, p. 24) (Figure 9.1).

PROFESSIONAL DEVELOPMENT IN A PROFESSIONAL DISCIPLINE

The early childhood (EC) discipline is responsible for the transformative education of babies and young children aged 0–8 years. Transformative education is defined as education that is based on 'the principles of empowerment, social justice, emancipation, and freedom' (McLeod, 2015, p. 256). As a developing graduate, your own professional development is essential to support the development of quality provision and the retention of staff. Significant evidence from Bonetti (2017) indicates that quality provision has a lasting impact on children and the likelihood that they will achieve their potential.

As EC practitioners, the workforce have become accustomed and frequently discuss practice and the adjustments needed to support children's growth and holistic development. All too often practitioners tend to neglect their own continuing professional development (CPD) and career aspirations due to long working hours and additional responsibilities (Ingleby, 2018).

Winton et al. (2016) argue for the importance of having CPD that provides the knowledge, skills and dispositions which can develop high-quality learning environments for children so that evidence-based practice can be implemented.

The graduate journey is a transformative process and genuine opportunities are required to engage in rich CPD and communities of practice. This helps to inspire, empower the workforce and help evolve practices for the benefit of practitioners, children and families. In order to value practitioners' expertise and recognise EC graduates as pedagogical leaders of practice, this journey begins with the graduate practitioner competencies although the demand for further political discussion is essential, as the responsibilities as a practitioner increase.

RECOGNISING THE EXPERTISE OF A GRADUATE EARLY CHILDHOOD GRADUATE PRACTITIONER

Honneth's (1995) theory of recognition helps to provoke discussions about how the EC workforce sees and promotes itself, and how wider society positions the value of the roles within the discipline. At this time, the EC sector would benefit from further recognition about the expertise and impact they have upon young children's lives. As a graduate practitioner you will be evolving as a critical thinker and representative of our profession.

REFLECTION

1. When you talk to friends and family about your role as an EC practitioner, how do you explain your roles and responsibilities?
   When thinking about your practice, do you use any of the following words?
   - Leading practice
   - Pedagogical expertise
   - Play based learning
   - Influencer and innovator
2. How would using these words to describe your practice make you feel?

DEVELOPING AS EARLY CHILDHOOD GRADUATE PRACTITIONERS (ECGP)

As a developing graduate professional, the ECGPCs will take you on a journey to help your confidence grow, and you will begin to see how the skills and competencies you have developed will impact upon the children's lives.

Figure 9.2 illustrates the learner journey through each year of a degree. It indicates the interconnection between the recognition we receive as citizens for the contribution we make to our society and the relationship we hold. One of the current debates in our discipline is the way that EC practitioners are viewed, valued and recognised as expert pedagogical practitioners.

Honneth's theory of recognition (1995) helps us to see how students on courses with ECGPCs develop their skills, knowledge and competencies as their degree progresses. Once you become a graduate professional, you will have expertise in a range of pedagogical, theoretical and practical knowledge.

The ECGPCs are a significant step key in promoting, positioning and recognising the expertise in the discipline while providing a theoretical platform to help empower practitioners and lead change within practice.

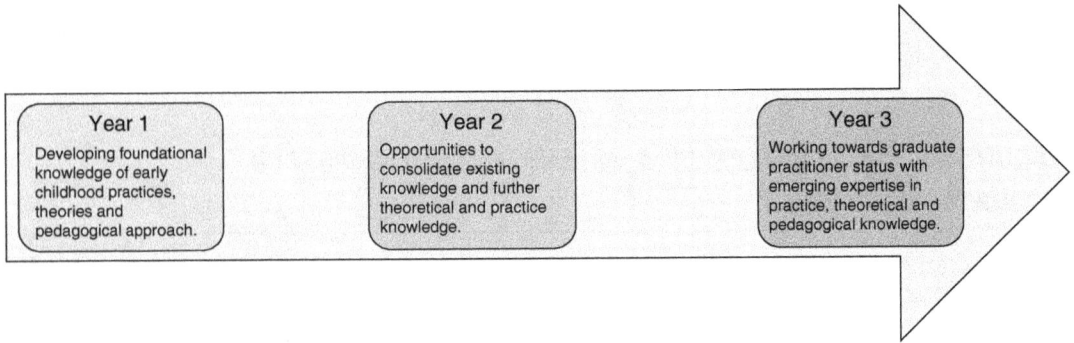

Year 1	Year 2	Year 3
Developing foundational knowledge of early childhood practices, theories and pedagogical approach.	Opportunities to consolidate existing knowledge and further theoretical and practice knowledge.	Working towards graduate practitioner status with emerging expertise in practice, theoretical and pedagogical knowledge.

Figure 9.2 Learner journey through graduate degree

HOW ECGPCS SUPPORT PROFESSIONAL DEVELOPMENT ONCE PRACTITIONERS HAVE GRADUATED

As a developing ECEC graduate, you will provide evidence and demonstrate your skills, knowledge and competencies over a period of time. Once you graduate, you will continually refine your practice and your understanding will be influenced by your experiences, interactions and relationships with others and your own professional reflections.

You will see in the table (see further reading section at the end of the chapter) that the Early Years Foundation Stage (EYFS) (DfE, 2022) has been identified alongside the frameworks for Wales, Scotland and Ireland. Keeping abreast of other nations' decisions and policy drivers is an important part of maintaining competency and being aware of pedagogical debates in the sector.

REFLECTING ON YOUR CURRENT PRACTICE

Evolving and changing practices are key aspects within our daily practices. As intuitive practitioners, you will instinctively know when something is not working for the children or families you work with. You may also be unsure how to make the necessary changes.

REFLECTION

1. Are there areas of practice that you would like to change?
2. Have you discussed your ideas with your colleagues?
3. Do you need to provide further information to help your colleagues understand your pedagogical ideas?
4. Where will you obtain the information from?
5. Is there an evidence base to help support your idea?
6. How do you plan to make the changes?

ACTIVITY: ACTION PLAN

Use the questions above to help you complete an action plan to develop your practice.

Practice to be changed	How will you achieve this?	What do you need to support you to achieve this?

Now you have identified action points; what order of priority would you do them?

The following case study allows you to explore how to work with others in ECEC settings to maximise the outcomes for children through challenging and influencing practice.

CASE STUDY 1: JASMINE (A RECENT GRADUATE)

Jasmine started working in a private day Nursery after graduation.

- *There are no other graduates in the setting currently.*
- *The main interests are focused upon early literacy and baby brain development (neuroscience).*
- *Jasmine worked in a pre-school during their level 3 qualification placement experiences but found this less rewarding than other age groups.*

The owner of Nursery was insistent that the graduate worked in the pre-school, rather than the baby room and the reason given was 'it would be better for Ofsted to see a graduate working with 4–5 years old to help get the best outcomes on the EYFS profile.'

REFLECTION

1. Is there value in the graduate working with the preschool, toddler or baby rooms?
2. How would you respectfully challenge the decisions being made?

(Continued)

(Continued)
3. How could the practitioner effectively assert their understanding about the value of working in the preferred age group?
4. What CPD would benefit the practitioner?
5. What skills and competencies does the graduate need to develop further?

DEVELOPING YOUR PRACTICE

Now you have responded to Case Study 1, let's explore how CPD can play a further role in developing as an ECEC graduate practitioner.

Some examples of CPD are listed below. These are not listed in order of importance as each has its own distinct value and this list is not exhaustive.

- Discussing ideas and sharing practice with colleagues both in and out of your place of work. This process might be informal, but it helps you to externalise your ideas and justify your decisions with people who understand the children and families you work with. This community is as unique as you are.
- Reading and listening to articles, journals, news reports, podcasts, blogs. Some good examples of these can be found at the end of the chapter.
- Engaging with politics and proposed changes to key policies. As an early childhood graduate practitioner, you can and should engage and comment upon proposed policy changes and Department for Education (DfE) consultations.
- Attend workshops, conferences, network meetings as and when possible. If you are unable, check the organisation website and You Tube channels as many organisations will record and share the presentations after the event.
- Set up your own professional network on social media to discuss current debates in the sector.
- Use the alumni network from your university to support you and access further training and CPD opportunities.

As you continue to develop your practice through CPD and reflection, your sense of professional identify will establish and evolve. We are now going to discuss this next below.

PROFESSIONAL IDENTITY

Professional identity is the image and perception we have of ourselves as experts in our field (Cruess, Cruess and Steinert, 2019). As practitioners in early childhood education and care, our identity can be defined by a range of professionals and regulatory bodies, including the DfE, ofsted, Social Work England and The Nursing and Midwifery Council. The identity of the ECEC practitioner goes beyond the roles and responsibilities described in the statutory framework for the Early Years Foundation Stage (EYFS) (DfE, 2021f), Social Work England's Professional Standards (SWE, 2021a) and the Nursing and Midwifery Council Standards (NMC, 2016). Professional identity for ECEC practitioners is about who we are rather than the role that we play and what makes us unique in our approach to ECEC (Lightwoot and Frost, 2015). Like the children we support, practitioners come in all shapes and sizes, each bringing their own experiences, skills and knowledge which we embed into our everyday practice.

BARRIERS TO RECOGNISING PROFESSIONAL IDENTITY

In ECEC, practitioners are often unable to acknowledge the high quality of attributes they possess as their focus is often on the children and the fulfilment of the generic job description, therefore dismissing the value and impact they have within the workforce. This could be partly due to perceptions of the role of practitioners is the ability to care for children, a generic understanding which does not begin to acknowledge the multi-faceted identity of the ECEC practitioner. Some researchers have even gone as far as to suggest ECEC practitioners are seen as glorified babysitters (Quinones, Barnes and Berger, 2021). This perception is naturally damning to the confidence of practitioners' own perceptions of their professional identity.

ACTIVITY: JOB DESCRIPTION

Think about all the things you do in setting as a developing graduate practitioner. Write a job description including all the things you do daily as an ECEC practitioner. You may want to use the example template below (Figure 9.3).

Early Childhood Practitioner - Job description

Job title	
Job description	
Required qualifications	
Duties and responsibilities	
Desired characteristics	
Required experience	
Desirable experience	

Figure 9.3 Developing your graduate practice

(Continued)

(Continued)

Now you have created your job description; compare this with published job descriptions of the same title.

REFLECTION

1. What are the differences between your job description and the one you have compared it to?
2. How has writing a job description helped you to recognise aspects of your own professional identity?

THE EXTENDED ROLE OF EARLY CHILDHOOD EDUCATION CARE PRACTITIONER

As ECEC practitioners, we not only have the ability to care for children but also alongside our day-to-day duties of planning for assessments, meeting the individual needs of the children, creating a safe and enabling environment; we also have the additional roles of supporting parents and families, developing the ECEC setting in which we work as well as making an impact in the wider community and workforce.

Recognising practitioners for the professional development which they have undertaken not only enhances their sense of self-esteem but also allows them to be recognised for their accomplishments which differentiate them from others (Peleman et al., 2018; Quinones et al., 2021).

To be able to manage this ever-growing job description as well as building confidence in their own abilities, it is important for practitioners to continuously develop and expand their thinking and their skills while gaining recognition for the work we do. CPD is highly individualistic and allows the practitioner to develop, think and interact in a way that demonstrates their abilities and securing their professional identity to themselves and others (Trodd and Dickerson, 2022).

REFLECTING ON YOUR PROFESSIONAL IDENTITY

As part of the development process for graduate practitioners, it is vital do develop as a reflective practitioner (Reed and Canning, 2010). The process of reflection helps build an understanding of what support and professional development is required to benefit and improve knowledge and practice. Reflection is key to understanding not only your needs but the needs of the children and the setting in which you work. Therefore, creating an ever-improving environment and high-quality provision and practice.

Through reflection, as a practitioner you can identify the key aspects of your professional practice which can be strengthened further as well as creating a continuous provision for improvement.

REFLECTION

1. What do you do well?
2. How will you continue to do that?
3. What support do you need to be the professional you can be?

CASE STUDY 2: GAVIN (AN EXPERIENCED PRACTITIONER)

Gavin's interests and skills are in the moment planning, play pedagogy and working with families. Gavin graduated 10 years ago and has worked in community practice as a volunteer and outreach work with families.

The outreach team leader suggested that working in the toddlers would be best as they were short staffed, due to changes in the wider team.

REFLECTION

1. How could the practitioner's skills be used to best advantage for both the practitioner and the children?
2. Is there value for the setting, practitioner and children for the practitioner to work with the toddlers? What evidence can you provide for this?
3. Which skills and competencies does the practitioner need to develop further?

APPLYING REFLECTION TO PRACTICE

In practice, reflection happens daily, without much thought or recognition of this fact. You will review a child's development or a planned activity and through reflection evaluate if the approach being taken is the best for you, the child and the setting and make the necessary changes to make it better. If you have a child with additional needs you are unfamiliar with, you will reflect on this and make changes to develop your practice to best support the child. It is as if reflection is embedded into our daily work and practice. However, the process of professional reflection is often difficult for practitioners to do. Many grapple with the concept of evaluating their own strengths and areas for development and often neglect to do this regularly or attempt to reflect but superficially. Only when deep meaningful reflection on our practice takes place, we can truly develop and grow as ECEC practitioners creating a strong workforce in ECEC. Through truly engaging in reflective development, you are actively engaging in life-long learning (Slade et al., 2019).

As discussed previously, CPD presents effective opportunities to reflect on and in practice which can be explored further through theoretical underpinning.

HISTORY AND POLICY CHANGES: DRIVE TO PROFESSIONALISE THE WORKFORCE

As identified elsewhere in this chapter, the EC sector incorporates a range of workers from different disciplines including health, social work, early education and community practice. Since the inception of such services, the notion of continuing to build up your professional practice has (at various points in history) been afforded credibility and value in practice. Concurrent government policies in the EC sector have suggested value associated with CPD opportunities. Each of these governments have demonstrated different policy priorities (particularly in relation to EC care and education) with ensuant legislation and policy initiatives placing an influence on the perceived impact of CPD opportunities for EC professionals. This is particularly evident in the EC sector which has been a voting battleground subject to significant changes since its original inception in the year 2000 (DfEE, 2000). While this element of the chapter considers the EC work sector, a greater focus is on EC practice because of the significant and far-reaching changes attributed to the value offered to CPD.

One way to better understand the history of policy changes in relation to CPD is to undertake a policy analysis. This is a type of academic writing you are likely to encounter at some point on your graduate learner journey. Policy analysis can be described in a variety of ways (Walt and Gilson, 1994) but for the purposes of this chapter, we are using this term to determine whether policies will achieve their proposed goals (Bardach, 2015).

What we present here is a partial policy analysis of key legislation, policy frameworks and guidance documents that have had and continue to have a direct influence on the goal of promoting and legislating for EC practitioners to have opportunities to engage with CPD. Garnering a better understanding of the influence of policy on practice (particularly around CPD) is likely to enhance our understanding of the shift that has occurred in the sector with a move away from the Mum's army towards a graduate-led workforce (Osgood, 2009).

The timeline shown in Figure 9.4 offers a brief overview of some policy, legislative documents and government commissioned reports.

A HISTORY OF CPD OPPORTUNITIES IN ECEC

As highlighted previously in this chapter, CPD is recognised (in various forms) in each iteration of the EYFS. Early versions of the EYFS (DfEE, 2000, 2003) were introduced at a time when government policies were focused on improving and expanding the early years workforce with a focus on improved qualifications and CPD opportunities. The second iteration of this framework recognised that good CPD opportunities for practitioners, leaders and managers would likely have a positive effect on staff morale and retention (DfEE, 2003). The 2003 version of the EYFS coincided with the introduction of the children's workforce unit who would be charged with increasing the availability of 'high quality, continuous professional development for all who work with children' (DfEE, 2003, p. 7).

Across the ECEC workforce, staff appraisals are an essential feature of the CPD cycle (DCSF, 2008). These present opportunities for managers/supervisors to identify the individual training needs of practitioners with a view to providing vigorous programmes of CPD to meet these

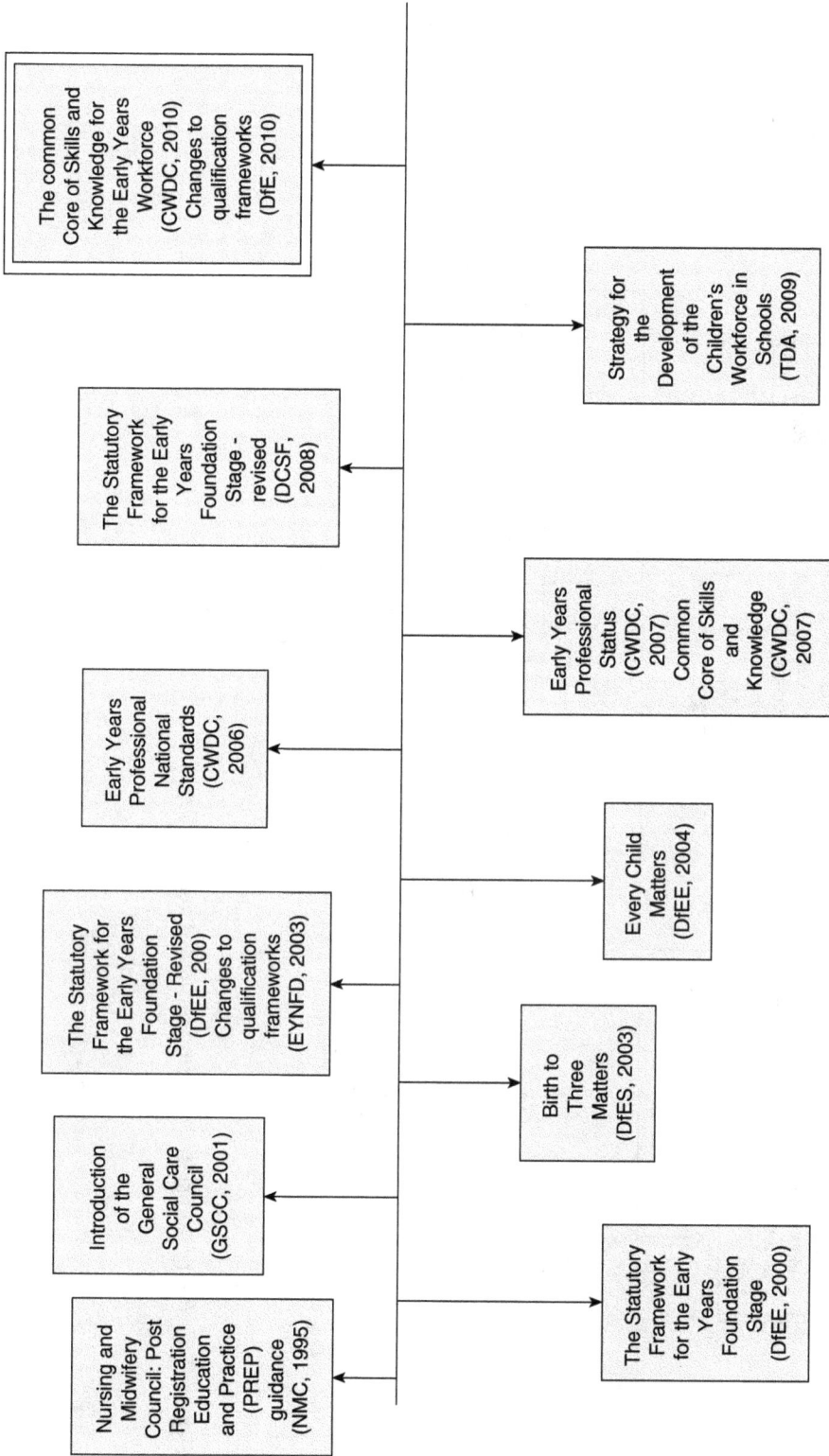

Figure 9.4 Policy, legislation and government reports timeline (*Continued*)

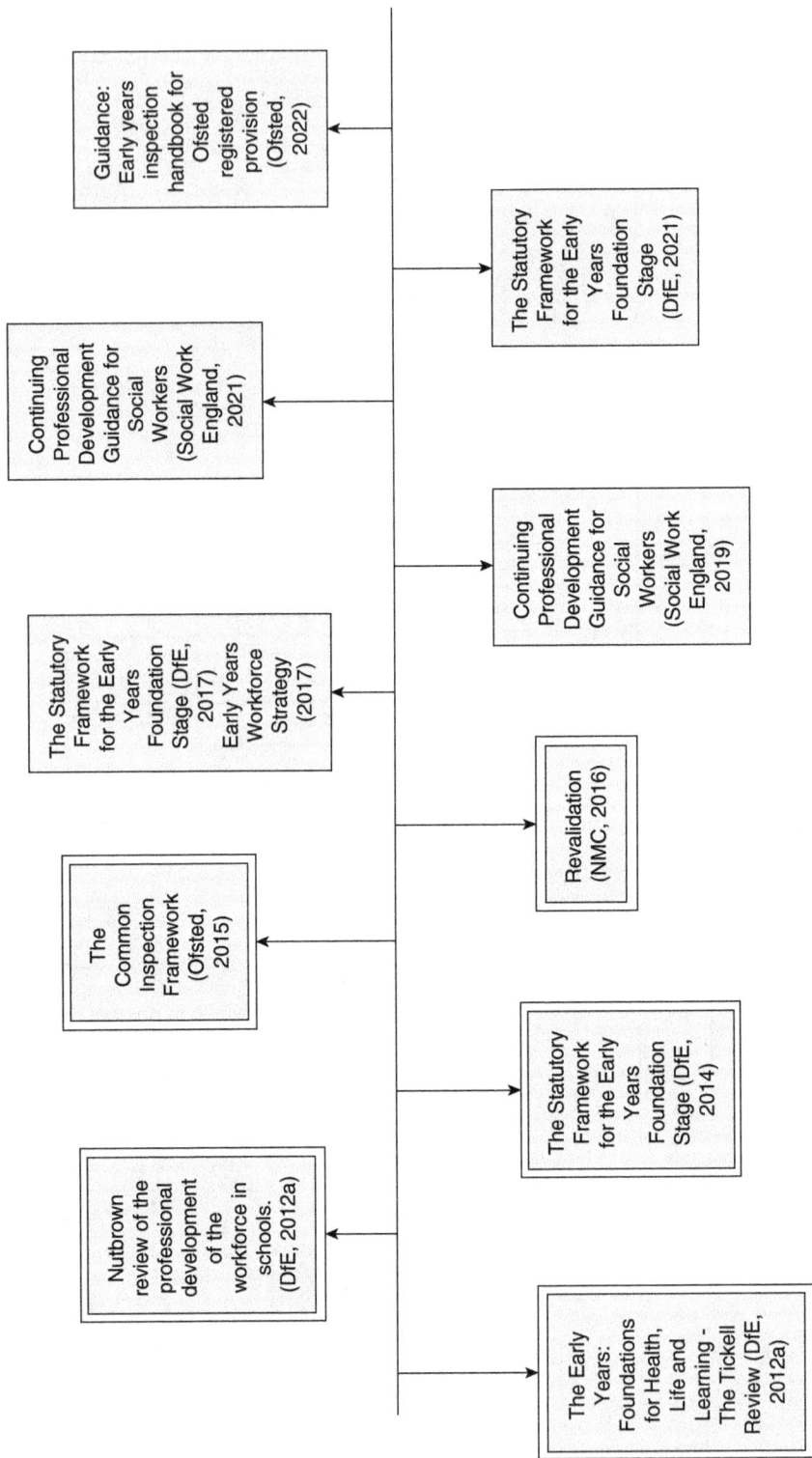

Figure 9.4 Policy, legislation and government reports timeline

needs. Within some EC sectors, practitioners are encouraged to work (initially) under professional supervision allowing them to learn from others who more experienced and established.

In 2014, the DfE provided further revisions to the EYFS and, for the first time, closely associated the learning and development opportunities of children with the qualification level, training skill and knowledge of EC practitioners. There was a shift in language used in this version of the framework with the modal verb 'must' being used for the first time in relation to CPD. The framework suggested that providers were obligated to 'support staff to undertake appropriate training and professional development opportunities to ensure they offer quality learning and development experiences for children that continually improves' (DfE, 2014, p. 20). The 2017 (DfE, 2017) and 2021 (DfE, 2021) versions of the framework repeated much of what had been said previously about the value of CPD, again, tying this to children's daily experiences and placing an obligation on providers to ensure the CPD needs of staff were satisfied.

ONLINE CPD

Earlier in this chapter, we provided a brief examination of the 'Foundations for Quality: The independent review of early education and childcare qualifications' (DfE, 2012b) and what its author had to say about CPD. One recommendation within this report was that settings might access online CPD opportunities which should be regulated to provide commonality and consistency across settings. The coalition government at the time of publication of this report did not adopt this recommendation and while there is no overall oversight of early years professional CPD online, plenty of quality CPD learning tools are available to practitioners. The NMC and SWE encourage a range of CPD learning opportunities and recognise that online CPD can be a valuable method of supporting CPD opportunities. This recognition of online learning opportunities recognises the growth in ICT usage in the United Kingdom.

Now you have come to the end of the chapter and considered your own graduate journey; it's no time to explore how CPD can support you to progress in your graduate roles.

REFLECTION

1. What are your CPD priorities over the next: three months, six months, a year?
2. How will you engage with other practitioners and professional to share your learning and experience as you progress through this CPD?
3. How will this CPD proposed impact on your own pedagogy and the quality outcomes of children?

CHAPTER SUMMARY

Throughout the chapter, there have been opportunities to consider your own professional practice and the way that you see and value CPD.

The chapter has discussed professional development alongside concepts of self-belief, self-respect and self-esteem. Hopefully, the chapter has provided you with some food for thought for both developing your own practice and leading change with those around you.

As a graduate practitioner you will need to continually manage your time to ensure that your own development is not a secondary consideration to everyone else's priorities. This can be hard to manage especially if you are new in your role. Your graduate skills and competencies will help you influence change, engage with evidenced-based research and provoke discussions about pedagogy.

Honneth's (1995) theory reminds us that we need to value our own contribution and project the significant role that we play in children and family's lives.

Remember to project that you are a developing graduate professional by actively engaging in the following:

- Self-belief – strive to be a critical reflective practitioner and make the best choices you can for the children and families you work with. You are experts in understanding the needs of the children.
- Self-esteem – when you talk about your role and responsibilities, help other people understand what you do and why your role is essential to help children's growth and development.
- Self-recognition – as a graduate practitioner, be clear that you have undergone a rigorous process to be awarded your GPC's. You should be proud of your degree and your GPCs.

The EC workforce will continue to face challenges and the next generation of graduates will help transform children's and families' lives. As a developing graduate you have a key role in marketing the importance of your role and the impact that you have upon children's outcomes.

REFERENCES

Allen, D. and Hulmes, A. (2021) Adverse racism and child protection practice with Gypsy, Roma and Traveller children and families. *Seen and Heard*, 31, 2.

Allen, G. (2011) *Early intervention: The next steps an independent report to Her Majesty's Government.* Available at: https://assets.publishing.service.gov.uk/government/uploads/system/uploads/attachment_data/file/284086/early-intervention-next-steps2.pdf [Accessed: 31 October 2022].

Alsop-Shields, L. and Mohay, H. (2001) *John Bowlby and James Roberston: Theorists, scientists and crusaders for improvements in the care of children in hospital.* [online] Available at: https://onlinelibrary.wiley.com/doi/epdf/10.1046/j.1365-2648.2001.01821.x [Accessed: 6 July 2022].

Armstrong, C. (2022) *My experience with the early childhood graduate practitioner competencies.* [online] Available at: sunderland.ac.uk

Bardach, E. (2015) *A practical guide for policy analysis: The eightfold path to more effective problem solving.* London: CQ Press.

Benford, J. and Tait, C. (2017) Working together in groups with parents of young children. Growing together at the Pen Green Centre. In M. Whalley (Ed.), *Involving parents in their children's learning: A knowledge-sharing approach.* London: Sage.

BERA/TACTYC (2017) *Early Childhood Research Review 2003–17.* London: British Educational Research Association. Available at: https://www.bera.ac.uk/project/bera-tactyc-early-childhood-research-review-2003-2017 [Accessed 14 June 2022].

Berger, P. L. and Luckman, T. (1966) *The social construction of reality: A treatise in the sociology of knowledge.* Garden City, NY: Anchor Books.

Bertram, T. and Pascal, C. (2016) *High Achieving White Working Class (HAWWC) Boys Project.* Centre for Research in Early Childhood. [online] Available at: www.crec.co.uk/research

Bhatt, T (2021) *The role of culture in early childhood development.* [online] Available at: https://novakdjokovicfoundation.org/the-role-of-culture-in-early-childhood-development/. [Accessed: 18 August 2022].

Birth to 5 Matters (2021) *Non statutory guidance for the early years foundation stage.* Available at: Birthto5Matters-download.pdf [Accessed: 6 May 2022].

Bollinger, M. E., Dahlquist, L. M., Mudd, K., Sonntag, C., Dillinger, L. and McKenna, K. (2006) The impact of food allergy on the daily activities of children and their families. *Annals of Allergy, Asthma, & Immunology*, 96(3), 415–421.

Bonetti (2017) *Analysis – Developing the early years workforce.* Available at: epi.org.uk

Boyd, D., Hirst, N. and Siraj-Blatchford, J. (2018) *Understanding sustainability in early childhood education: Case studies and approaches from across the UK.* Oxon: Routledge.

Bradbury, A. (2022) Valerie Daniel. In A. Bradbury and R. Swailes (Eds.), *Early childhood theories today* (p. 116). London: Learning Matters.

Bradbury, A. (2022) Nurturing in the early years: What the science tells us. *Early Education*, 69. ISSN 0960–281X

Bradbury, A. and Swailes, R. (2022) *Early childhood theories today.* London: Learning Matters.

Bristow, K., Capewell, S., Abba, K. and Lloyd-Williams, F. (2011) Healthy eating in early years settings: A review of current national to local guidance for Northwest England. *Public Health Nutrition*, 14(6), 1008–1016. Available at: https://doi.org/10.1017/S1368980010003836

Brodie, K. (2018) *The Holistic Care and Development of Children from Birth to Three. An essential guide for students and practitioners.* London: Routledge.

Bronfenbrenner, U. (1979) *The ecology of human development: Experiments by nature and design.* Cambridge: Harvard University Press.

Bronfenbrenner, U. (1986) Ecology of the family as a context for human development: Research perspectives. *Developmental Psychology*, 22(6), 723–742.

Bronfenbrenner, U. (1990) *Who cares for children?* (pp.27–40). UNESCO. [Online] Available at: https://eprints.lib.hokudai.ac.jp/dspace/bitstream/2115/25254/1/12_P27-40.pdf [Accessed on: 23 October 2022].

Bronfenbrenner, U. (1992). Ecological systems theory. In R. Vasta (ed.), *Annals of child development. Six theories of child development: Revised formulations and current issues* (pp. 187–249). London: Jessica Kingsley.

Bronfenbrenner, U. (1994a) Ecological models of human development. In T. Husen and T. Postlethwaite (Eds.), *International encyclopedia of education* (Vol. 3, 2nd edn., 1643–1647). Oxford: Pergamon Press.

Bronfenbrenner, U. (1994b) Ecological models of human development. In *International encyclopaedia of education* (Vol. 3, 2nd edn.). Oxford: Elsevier.

Bronfenbrenner, U. (2005). *Making human beings human.* Thousand Oaks, CA: Sage.

Bruce, T. (1991) *A time to play in early education.* London: Hodder Education.

Burgess-Macey, C., Kelly, C. and Ouvry, M. (2020) Rethinking early years: How the neoliberal agenda fails children, soundings, 6. Available at: https://doi.org/10.3898/SOUN.76.09.2020

Cazaly, H. (2022) *Young children's health and wellbeing. From birth to 11.* London: Learning Matters.

Center on the Developing Child at Harvard University (2019) *What are ACES's and how do they relate to toxic stress.* Available at: https://developingchild.harvard.edu/resources/aces-and-toxic-stress-frequently-asked-questions/ [Accessed: 15 August 2022].

Center on the Developing Child: Harvard University (2022) *Resource library.* Available at: https://developingchild.harvard.edu/resources/ [Accessed 22 December 2022].

Charlesworth, R. (2016) *Understanding child development.* London: Sage.

Children Act 1989. Available at: http://www.legislation.gov.uk/ukpga/1989/41/contents [Accessed: 15 August 2022].

Children Act 2004. Available at: https://www.legislation.gov.uk/ukpga/2004/31/contents [Accessed: 15 August 2022].

Children and Social Care Act 2017. Available at: http://www.legislation.gov.uk/ukpga/2017/16/contents/enacted [Accessed: 15 August 2022].

Children's Alliance (2022) 4 Reports. Available at: https://childrensalliance.org.uk/working-group-reports/ [Accessed: 5 December 2022].

Children's Parliament (2021) *Rights based practice in the Early Years.* [Online] Available at: https://www.childrensparliament.org.uk/rights-based-early-years/ [Accessed: 31 August 2022].

Chilvers, D. (2018, Spring) Professionalising the process of observation and understanding children's development. *Early Education Journal.* Early Education.org. [Accessed: 19 September 2022].

Christensen, J. (2016) A critical reflection of Bronfenbrenner's development ecology model. *Problems of Education in the 21st Century*, 69(1), 22–28.

Clark, A. (2004) The mosaic approach and research with young children. In V. Lewis, M. Kellet and C. Robinson (Eds.), *The reality of research with children and young people.* London: Sage.

Cohen, B. L., Noone, S., Muñoz-Furlong, A. and Sicherer, S. H. (2004) Development of a questionnaire to measure quality of life in families with a child with food allergy. *Journal of Allergy and Clinical Immunology*, 114(5), 1159–1163.

Conkbayir, M. and Pascal, C. (2015) *Early childhood theories and contemporary issues. An introduction.* London: Bloomsbury.

Conkbayir, M. (2021) *Early childhood and neuroscience: Theory, research and implications for practice.* London: Bloomsbury.

Cruess, S. R., Cruess, R. L. and Steinert, Y. (2019) Supporting the development of a professional identity: General principles. *Medical Teacher*, 41(6), 641–649. Available at: https://doi.org/10.1080/0142159X.2018.1536260

Dalzell, R., Watson, A. and Massey, K. (2009) *A report on the Early Learning Partnership Project.* London: Family and Parenting Institute.

Department for Education (2020) *Critical workers and vulnerable children who can access schools or educational settings.* Available at: https://www.gov.uk/government/publications/coronavirus-covid-19-maintaining-educational-provision [Accessed: 12 July 2022].

Department of Health (2003) *Getting the right start: National Service Framework for Children Standard for Hospital Services.* Available at: https://assets.publishing.service.gov.uk/government/uploads/system/uploads/attachment_data/file/199953/Getting_the_right_start_-_National_Service_Framework_for_Children_Standard_for_Hospital_Services.pdf [Accessed: 07 June 2022].

DfE (2012a) *The early years: Foundations for life, health and learning: An independent report on the early years foundation stage to Her Majesty's government.* London: Crown Copyright.

DfE (2012b) *Nutbrown review of professional development of the children's workforce in schools.* London: Crown Copyright.

DfE (2014) *Statutory guidance for the early years foundation stage.* London: Crown Copyright.

DfE (2020) *Multi-agency statutory guidance on female genital mutilation.* London: DfE. Available at: https://www.gov.uk/government/publications/multi-agency-statutory-guidance-on-female-genital-mutilation [Accessed: 15 August 2022].

DfE (2021a) *Early years foundation stage (EYFS) statutory framework.* Available at: https://assets.publishing.service.gov.uk/government/uploads/system/uploads/attachment_data/file/974907/EYFS_-framework_-_March_2021.pdf [Accessed: 3 January 2023].

DfE (2021b) *Early years foundation stage (EYFS) statutory framework.* London: DfE. Available at: https://www.gov.uk/government/publications/early-years-foundation-stage-framework–2 [Accessed: 15 August 2022].

DfE (2021c) *Revised prevent duty Guidance: For England and Wales.* London: DfE. Available at: https://www.gov.uk/government/publications/prevent-duty-guidance/revised-prevent-duty-guidance-for-england-and-wales#contents [Accessed: 15 August 2022].

DfE (2021d) *Sexual violence and sexual harassment between children in schools and colleges.* Available at: https://www.gov.uk/government/publications/sexual-violence-and-sexual-harassment-between-children-in-schools-and-colleges [Accessed: 15 August 2022].

DfE (2021e) *Statutory guidance for the early years foundation stage.* London: Crown Copyright.

DfE (2021f) *Statutory framework for the early years foundation stage.* [Online] Available at: https://assets.publishing.service.gov.uk/government/uploads/system/uploads/attachment_data/file/974907/EYFS_framework

DfE (2021g) *Development matters non-statutory curriculum guidance for the early years foundation stage.* Available at: https://assets.publishing.service.gov.uk/government/uploads/system/uploads/attachment_-data/file/1007446/6.7534_DfE_Development_Matters_Report_and_illustrations_web__2_.pdf

DfE (2022) *Domestic abuse statutory guidance.* London: DfE. Available at: https://assets.publishing.service.gov.uk/government/uploads/system/uploads/attachment_data/file/1089015/Domestic_Abuse_Act_2021_Statutory_Guidance.pdf [Accessed: 15 August 2022].

DfE (2022) *Keeping children safe in education.* London: DfE. Available at: https://www.gov.uk/government/publications/keeping-children-safe-in-education–2 [Accessed: 15 August 2022].

DfEa (2021) *Statutory framework for the early years foundation stage.* [Online] Available at: https://assets.publishing.service.gov.uk/government/uploads/system/uploads/attachment_data/file/974907/EYFS_framework_-_March_2021.pdf [Accessed: 31 August 2022].

DfEb (2021) *Development matters: non-statutory curriculum guidance for the early years foundation stage.* Available at: https://assets.publishing.service.gov.uk/government/uploads/system/uploads/attachment_data/file/1007446/6.7534_DfE_Development_Matters_Report_and_illustrations_web__2_.pdf

DfEE (2000) *Statutory guidance for the early years foundation stage.* London: Crown Copyright.

DfEE (2003) *Statutory guidance for the early years foundation stage.* London: Crown Copyright.

Doherty, J. and Hughes, M. (2014) *Child development. Theory and practice 0–11* (2nd edn.). Harlow UK Pearson.

Duffy, B. and Pugh, G. (2013) Contemporary issues in the early years. *Contemporary Issues in the Early Years,* 1–320.

Dyer, M. and Taylor, S. (2012) Supporting professional identity in undergraduate Early Years students through reflective practice. *Reflective Practice,* 13(4), 551–563. Available at: https://doi.org/10.1080/14623943.2012.670620

Early Childhood Studies Competencies (2020) *Early childhood graduate practitioner competencies.* Available at: https://www.ecsdn.org/wp-content/uploads/2021/02/ECSDN-Early-Childhood-Graduate-Practitioner-Competencies-July-2020.pdf [Accessed: 15 June 2022].

Early Childhood Studies Degree Network (ECSDN) (2020) *Striving for excellence, early childhood graduate practitioner competencies.* England: ECSDN. Available at: https://www.ecsdn.org/competencies

Early Intervention Foundation (2022) *Why intervention matters.* Available at: https://www.eif.org.uk/why-it-matters/why-is-it-good-for-children-and-families [Accessed: 20 August 2022].

Early Intervention Foundation (N.D.) *What is early intervention?* [Online] Available at: https://www.eif.org.uk/why-it-matters/what-is-early-intervention [Accessed: 30 September 2022].

Early Years Coalition (2021) *Birth to 5 Matters: Non-statutory guidance for the early years foundation stage.* St Albans: Early Education. Available at: https://birthto5matters.org.uk/wp-content/uploads/2021/04/Birthto5Matters-download.pdf [Accessed: 3 January 2023].

Ellis, K. (2015) One moment in time: The transitory and concrete value of disability toys. In K. Ellis (Ed.), *Disability and popular culture: Focusing passion, creating community and expressing defiance* (15–34). Burlington: Ashgate.

Ephgrave, A. (2018) *Planning in the moment with young children: A practical guide for early years practitioners and parents* (1st edn.). London: Routledge.

Fairchild, N., Mikuska, E., Sabine, A. and Barton, S. (2022) The early childhood education and care sector's perspective on the early childhood studies graduate and the early childhood graduate practitioner competencies. Available at: https://www.researchgate.net/publication/365670728_The_Early_Childhood_Education_and_Care_sector%27s_perspective_on_the_Early_Childhood_Studies_-graduate_and_the_Early_Childhood_Graduate_Practitioner_Competencies [Accessed: 4 January 2023].

Favazza, P. C. and Siperstein, G. N. (2016) Motor skill acquisition for young children with disabilities. In B. Reichow, B. Boyd, E. Barton and S. Odom (Eds.), *Handbook of early childhood special education.* Cham: Springer. Available at: https://doi.org/10.1007/978-3-319-28492-7_13

Fisher, J. (2019) *Leading or following children's learning: A critical review of contradictory discourses in the role of early childhood educators.* Oxford Brookes University. Available at: https://ethos.bl.uk/OrderDetails.do?uin=uk.bl.ethos.800191.

Freeman, M. and Mathison, S. (2009) *Researching children's experiences.* London: Guildford Press.

Gov.UK (2022) *Meeting the needs of all children.* [Online] Available at: https://help-for-early-years-providers.education.gov.uk/get-help-to-improve-your-practice/meeting-the-needs-of-all-children [Accessed: 19 September 2022].

Great Ormond Street (2021) *The power of play.* [Online] Available at: https://media.gosh.org/documents/Power_of_Play_Report.pdf?_ga=2.169110501.530708877.1657104041-1110678657.1644428793 [Accessed: 06 July 2022].

Grimmer, T. (2021) *Developing a loving pedagogy in the early years: How love fits with professional practice.* Abingdon, Oxfordshire: Routledge.

Grimmer, T. (2022) Urie Bronfenbrenner (1917–2005). In A. Bradbury and R. Swailes (Eds.), *Early childhood theories today* (pp. 23–25). London: Learning Matters.

Gulyurtlu, S., Jacobs, N. and Evans, I. (2020) *The impact of children's play in hospital.* [Online] Available at: https://www.starlight.org.uk/wp-content/uploads/2020/10/Starlight_ImpactOfPlay_Report_Oct20.pdf [Accessed: 23 June 2022].

Hambrick, E., Brawner, T. W. and Perry, B. D. (2019) *Timing of early-life stress and the development of brain-related capacities.* [Online] Available at: https://www.frontiersin.org/articles/10.3389/fnbeh.2019.00183/full [Accessed: 28 June 22].

Hamilton, P. (2021). *Diversity and marginalisation in childhood: A guide for inclusive thinking 0–11.* London: Sage Publishing.

Hart, R. A. (1992) *Children's participation, from tokenism to participation.* Florence: UNICEF. [Online] Available at: https://www.unicef-irc.org/publications/pdf/childrens_participation.pdf [Accessed: 31 August 2022].

Harvard University (2014) *Excessive stress disrupts the architecture of the developing brain.* [Online] Available at: https://developingchild.harvard.edu/wp-content/uploads/2005/05/Stress_Disrupts_Architecture_Developing_Brain-1.pdf [Accessed: 7 July 2022].

Hasan, A. (2007) Public policy in early childhood education and care. *International Journal of Child care and education Policy,* 1(1), 1.

Healthcare Play Specialist Education Trust (2015) *Children's Environments of Care Report.* [Online] Available at: https://www.hpset.org.uk/downloads/research_development/HPSET_CEC%20Report.pdf [Accessed: 18 June 2022].

HMSO (1978) *The Warnock Report: Report of the committee of enquiry into the education of handicapped children and young people.* London: Her Majesty's Stationery Office.

Honneth, A. (2009). Anxiety and politics: The strengths and weaknesses of Franz Neumann's diagnosis of a social pathology. In *Pathologies of reason. On the legacy of critical theory* (pp. 146–156). New York: Columbia.

Howard, J. and McInnes, K. (2012) The impact of children's perception of an activity as play rather than not play on emotional well-being. *Child: Care, Health and Development* 39(5), 737–742.

Ingleby (2018) *Early years educators' perceptions of professional development in England: An exploratory study of p.* Available at: oclc.org

Joyce, R. (2012) *Outdoor learning: Past and present.* London: Sage.

Kanyal, M. (2014) *Children's Rights 0 – 8: Promoting participation in education and care.* Abingdon: Routledge.

Keeping children safe in education 2022 (DfE 2022) (1 September 2022) *Statutory guidance for schools and colleges.* [Online] Available at: https://assets.publishing.service.gov.uk/government/uploads/system/uploads/attachment_data/file/1101454/Keeping_children_safe_in_education_2022.pdf

Laevers, F. (2000) Forward to basics! Deep-level-learning and the experiential approach. *Early Years,* 20(2), 20–29.

Lave, J. and Wenger, E. (1991) *Situated learning: Legitimate peripheral participation.* Cambridge: Cambridge University Press.

Learning and Teaching Scotland (2010) *Pre-birth to three: Positive outcomes for Scotland's children and families.* [Online] Available at: https://stramash.org.uk/wp-content/uploads/2018/08/elc2_prebirthtothreebooklet.pdf [Accessed: 31 August 22].

Lightwood, S. and Frost, D. (2015) The professional identity of early years educators in England: Implications for a transformative approach to continuing professional development. *Professional Development in Education,* 41(2), 401–418.

Livingstone, S. (2016) Reframing media effects in terms of children's rights in the digital age. *Journal of Children and Media,* 10(1), 4–12. Available at: https://doi.org/10.1080/17482798.2015.1123164

Lumsden, E. (2018) *Child protection in the early years. A practical guide.* London: Jessica Kingsley Publishers.

Lynch, E. W. and Hanson, M. W. (2004) *Developing cross-cultural competence: A guide for working with children and their families* (3rd edn.). Baltimore, MD: Paul H. Brookes.

Mac Naughton, G. and Hughes, P. (2009) *Doing action research in early childhood studies: A step-by-step guide.* Maidenhead: Open University Press.

Martin, F. and Griffiths, H. (2014) Relating to the 'Other': Transformative, inter-cultural learning in post-colonial contexts. *Compare: A Journal of Comparative and International Education.* 44(6), 938–959.

McAfee (2022) *Cyberbullying in plain sight a McAfee connected family report*. Available at: https://www.mcafee.com/content/dam/consumer/en-us/docs/reports/rp-cyberbullying-in-plain-sight-2022-global.pdf [Accessed: 15 August 2022].

McAfee (2022) *New global McAfee cyberbullying report reveals children now regularly face threats of racism and physical harm*. [Online] Available at: https://www.mcafee.com/en-us/consumer-corporate/newsroom/press-releases/press-release.html?news_id=d1da63d3-47bd-48c1-9463-35a4d97799ba [Accessed: 15 August 2022].

McLeod, N. (2015) Reflecting on reflection: Improving teachers' readiness to facilitate participatory learning with young children. *Professional Development in Education*, 41(2), 254–272.

Meggit, C., Bruce, T. and Manning-Morton, J. (2016) *Childcare and education* (6th edn.). Oxon Hodder Education.

Mercer, J. A. (2018). *Child development: Concepts and theories*. London: Sage.

Moll, L., Amanti, C., Neff, D. and Gonzalez, N. (1992) Funds of knowledge for teaching: Using a qualitative approach to connect homes and classrooms. *Theory into Practice*, 31(2), 132–141.

Moore, J. (2022) *Developing secure attachment through play: helping vulnerable children to build their social and emotional wellbeing*. Oxfordshire: Routledge.

Morrow, V. and Richards, R. (1996) The ethics of social research with children: An overview. *Children and Society*, 10, 90–105.

Moss, P. (2014) Early childhood policy in England 1997–2013: Anatomy of a missed opportunity. *International Journal of Early Years Education*, 22(4), 346–358.

Murphy, K. (2022) *A guide to SEND in the early years*. Dublin: Bloomsbury Publishing.

Murray, J., Swadener, B. B. and Smith, K. (2019) *The Routledge international handbook of young children's rights*. London: Routledge. Available at: https://doi.org/10.4324/9780367142025

Musgrave, J. (2019) Reflexivity in research. In: Z. Brown and H. Perkins (Eds.), *Beyond the conventional: Using innovative methods in early years research*. Abingdon: Routledge.

Musgrave, J. and Stobbs, N. (2015) *Early years placements. A critical guide to outstanding work-based learning*. St Albans: Herts: Critical Publishing.

Musgrave, J. (2017) *Supporting children's health and wellbeing*. London: Sage.

Musgrave, J. (2019, August) Promoting young children's health: Putting it into practice. *Parenta Magazine*. Available at: https://www.parenta.com/2019/08/01/promoting-young-childrens-health-putting-it-in-to-practice/

Musgrave, J. (2021) Children's health and wellbeing. In I. Palaiologou (Ed.), *The early years foundation stage: Theory and practice* (4th edn.). London: Sage.

Musgrave, J. and Payler, J. (2021) *Proposing a model for promoting children's health in early childhood education and care settings*. Children and Society. Available at: https://onlinelibrary.wiley.com/doi/full/10.1111/chso.12449

Nolan, A. and Molla, T. (2018) Teacher professional learning in early childhood education: Insights from a mentoring program. *Early Years*, 38(3), 258–270. Available at: https://doi.org/10.1080/09575146.2016.1259212

National Autistic Society (2022) National Autistic Society. Available at: https://www.autism.org.uk/ [Accessed: 7 April 2023].

National Institute for Health and Care Excellence (2022) *Children and young people products*. Available at: https://www.nice.org.uk/guidance/population-groups/children-and-young-people/products?Status=''' Published [Accessed: 5 December 2022].

Neaum, S. (2022) *Child development for early years students and practitioners* (5th edn.). London: Learning Matters.

Nguyen, T., Cheruvu, T. and Cheruvu, R. (2020) 'Childhood innocence for settler children: Disrupting colonialism and innocence in early childhood curriculum', *The New Educator*, 16(2), 131–148.

NMC (2016) *RCN Factsheet: Continuing Professional Development (CPD) for Nurses Working in the United Kingdom (UK)*. London: NMC.

NSPCC Learning (2022) Available at: https://learning.nspcc.org.uk/safeguarding-child-protection. [Accessed: 15 August 2022].

Nutbrown, C, Clough, P. and Atherton, F. (2013) *Inclusion in the early years.* London: Sage.

Nutbrown, C. (2012) *Foundations for quality: The independent review of early education and childcare qualifications.* Final report. Available at: https://assets.publishing.service.gov.uk/government/uploads/system/uploads/attachment_data/file/175463/Nutbrown-Review.pdf [Accessed: 3 January 2023].

Nutbrown, C. and Atherton, F. (2013) Understanding schemas and young children: From birth to three. *Understanding Schemas and Young.*

Ofsted (2022) *Research and analysis: Education recovery in early years providers.* GOV.UK. Available at: https://www.gov.uk/government/publications/early-years-inspection-handbook-eif/early-years-inspection-handbook-for-ofsted-registered-provision-for-september-2021 [Accessed: 3 January 2023].

Ofsted (2022) *Early years inspection handbook for Ofsted-registered provision.* [Online] Available at: https://www.gov.uk/government/publications/early-years-inspection-handbook-eif/early-years-inspection-handbook-for-ofsted-registered-provision-for-september-2021#print-or-save-to-pdf [Accessed: 31 August 2022].

Olsson, L. M. (2009) *Movement and experimentation in young children's learning: Deleuze and Guattari in early childhood education.* London: Routledge.

Osgood, J. (2009) Childcare workforce reform in England and 'the early years professional': A critical discourse analysis. *Journal of Education Policy,* 24(6), 733–751.

Pacini-Ketchabaw, V., Kind, S. and Kocher, L. (2017) *Encounters with materials in early childhood education.* London: Routledge.

Page, J. (2017). Reframing infant-toddler pedagogy through a lens of professional love: Exploring narratives of professional practice in early childhood settings in England. *Contemporary Issues in Early Childhood,* 18(4), 387–399. https://doi.org/10.1177/14639491177427.

Parten, M. B. (1933). Social play among preschool children. *Journal of Abnormal and Social Psychology,* 28(2), 136–147. Available at: https://doi.org/10.1037/h0073939 [Accessed: 7 April 2023].

Pascal, C., Bertram, T. and Rouse, L. (2019) *Getting it right in the early years foundation stage: A review of the evidence.* [Online] Available at: https://early-education.org.uk/wp-content/uploads/2021/12/Getting-it-right-in-the-EYFS-Literature-Review.pdf [Accessed: 19 October 2022].

Peleman, B., Lazzari, A., Budginaite, I., Siarova, H., Hauari, H., Peeters, J. and Cameron, C. (2018) Continuous professional development and ECEC quality: Findings from European systematic literature review. *European Journal of Education,* 53, 9–22. Available at: https://doi.org/10.1111/ejed.12257

Piaget, J. (1962). *Play, dreams, and imitation in childhood.* New York: Norton.

Pirbhai-Illich, F. and Martin, F. (2020) Understanding hospitality and invitation as dimensions of decolonising pedagogies when working interculturally. In P. Bamber (Ed.), *Teacher education for sustainable development and global citizenship.* New York, NY: Routledge.

Platt, H. (1959) *The welfare of children in hospital.* London: Ministry of Health, Central Health Services Council.

Powell, T. (2019) *Early intervention.* Briefing Paper. Number 7647. London: House of Commons Library.

Professional learning, Research in Social Sciences and Technology, Vol. 5 No. 1, pp. 22–44.

Public Health England (2017) *Example menus for early years settings in England.* Available at: https://assets.publishing.service.gov.uk/government/uploads/system/uploads/attachment_data/file/658870/Early_years_menus_part_1_guidance.pdf [Accessed: 1 November 2022].

Public Health England (2021) *Best start in life and beyond. Guidance to support commissioning of the healthy child programme.* Available at: https://assets.publishing.service.gov.uk/government/uploads/system/uploads/attachment_data/file/969168/Commissioning_guide_1.pdf [Accessed: 23 December 2022].

QAA (2022) *Subject Benchmark statements: Early childhood studies.* [Online] Available at: http://file/C:/Users/u22987/Downloads/sbs-early-childhood-studies-22%20(3).pdf [Accessed: 31 August 2022].

Quinones, G., Barnes, M. and Berger, E. (2021) Early childhood educators' solidarity and struggles for recognition. *Australasian Journal of Early Childhood*, 46(4), 296–308. Available at: https://doi.org/10.1177/18369391211050165

Quintana, S. M. (2010) Ethnicity, race and children's social development. In P. K. Smith and C. H. Hart (Eds.), *The Wiley-Blackwell handbook of childhood social development* (2nd edn., pp. 231–239).

Qvortrup, J. (1994) Childhood matters: An introduction. In J. Qvortrup, M. Bardy, G. Sgritta and H. Wintersberge (Eds.), *Childhood matters: Social theory, practice and politics* (pp. 1–23). Brookfield, VT: Aveburg.

Ramsden, S. (2010) *Practical approaches to co-production: Building effective partnerships with people using services, carers, families and citizens.* London: Department of Health.

Reed, M. and Canning, N. (2010) *Reflective practice in the early years.* London: Sage.

Rinaldi, C. (2006) *In dialogue with Reggio Emilia: Listening, researching, and learning.* London: Routledge.

Robson, S. and Zachariou, A. (2022) *Self-regulation in the early years.* London: Learning Matters.

Rogoff, B. (2003) *The cultural nature of human development.* New york, NY: Oxford University Press.

Royal College of Paediatrics and Child Health (2020) *State of child health 2020.* [Online] Available at: https://www.rcpch.ac.uk/resources/state-of-child-health [Accessed: 18 June 2022].

Saracho, O. N. (2021) Theories of child development and their impact on early childhood education and care. *Early Childhood Education Journal.* [Online] Available at: https://link.springer.com/article/10.1007/s10643-021-01271-5 [Accessed: 19 September 2022].

Scottish Childminding Association (2016) *Child-led participation.* [Online] Available at: https://www.careinspectorate.com/images/documents/News/Child_Led_Participation_Guide.pdf [Accessed: 31 August 2022].

Shier, H. (2001) Pathways to participation: Openings, opportunities and obligations. *Children & Society*, 15, 107–117. Available at: https://doi.org/10.1002/chi.617.

Sinaga, L., Siburian, P. and Siburian, P. (2020). The impact of parent class on parent Engagement in children's education. In *Proceedings of the First Nommensen International Conference on Creativity & Technology, NICCT, 20–21 September 2019, Medan, North Sumatera, Indonesia.*

Siraj-Blatchford, J., and Brock, L. (2016) *Putting the Schema back into schema theory and practice: An introduction to SchemaPlay.* SchemaPlay Publications.

Slade, M., Burnham, T., Catalana, S. and Waters, T. (2019) The impact of reflective practice on teacher candidates' learning. *International Journal for the Scholarship of Teaching and Learning.* 13(2), 1–8. Available at: https://doi.org/10.20429/ijsotl.2019.130215

Smidt, S. (2010) *Playing to learn: The role of play in the early years.* London: Taylor & Francis Group.

Society, N. A. (2022) *National Autistic Society, National Autistic Society.* Available at: https://www.autism.org.uk/ [Accessed: 7 April 2023].

Statham, J. and Chase, E. (2010) *Child wellbeing: A brief overview.* Available at: https://assets.publishing.service.gov.uk/government/uploads/system/uploads/attachment_data/file/183197/Child-Wellbeing-Brief.pdf [Accessed: 23 December 2022].

Style, E. (1988) Curriculum as window and Mirror. In D. Flinders and S. Thornton (Eds.), *Listening for all voices: Gender Balancing the school curriculum* (pp. 6–12). Summit: Oak Knoll.

SWE (2021a) *The professional standards.* Available at: https://www.socialworkengland.org.uk/standards/professional-standards/ [Accessed: 10 June 2022].

SWE (2021b) *CPD guidance.* Available at: https://www.socialworkengland.org.uk/cpd/cpd-guidance/ [Accessed: 10 June 2022].

Thomas, N., Crowley, A., Moxon, D., Ridley, J., Street, C. and Joshi, P. (2017) Independent advocacy for children and young people: Developing an outcomes framework. *Children & Society*, 31(5), 365–377. Available at: https://doi.org/10.1111/chso.12207

Tonkin, A. (2014) *The provision of play in health service delivery: Fulfilling children's rights under article 31 of the United Nations convention on the rights of the child.* [Online] Available at: https://www.england.nhs.uk/6cs/wp-content/uploads/sites/25/2015/03/nahps-full-report.pdf [Accessed: 17 June 2022].

UN CRC (1989) *The United Nations Convention on the Rights of the Child.* [Online] Available at: https://www.unicef.org.uk/rights-respecting-schools/wp-content/uploads/sites/4/2017/01/UNCRC-in-full.pdf [Accessed: 31 August 2022].

UNCRC (1989) *United Nation Convention of the Rights of the Child.* [online] Available at: http://www.ohchr.org/en/professionalinterest/pages/crc.aspx.

UNICEF (1989) *The United Nations Convention on the Rights of the Child.* [Online] Available at: https://www.unicef.org.uk.

UNICEF. (2021) *The State of the World's Children 2021: Promoting, protecting and caring for children's mental health.* Available at: https://www.unicef.org/media/114636/file/SOWC-2021-full-report-English.pdf [Accessed 10 July 22].

United Nations (20 November 1989) Convention on the Rights of the Child. General Assembly Resolution 44/25, UN Doc. A/RES/44/25. UN.

Walker, G. (2018) *Working together for children: A critical approach to multi-agency working.* London: Bloomsbury Academic.

Wall, S., Litjens, I. and Taguma, M. (2015) *Early childhood education and care pedagogy review: England.* [Online] Available at: https://www.oecd.org/unitedkingdom/early-childhood-education-and-care-pedagogy-review-england.pdf [Accessed: 26 September 2022].

Walt, G. and Gilson, L. (1994). Reforming the health sector in developing countries: The central role of policy analysis. *Health Policy and Planning*, 9, 353–370.

Wenger, E. (1998) *Communities of practice: Learning, meaning, and identity.* Cambridge: Cambridge University Press.

Whalley, M. and The Pen Green Centre Team (Ed.). (2017). *Involving parents in their children's learning: A knowledge-sharing approach.* London: Sage.

White, J. (2014) Ecological identity-values, principles and practice. In Duckett, R. and Drummond, M. J. (Eds.), *Learning to learn in nature.* Sightlines Initiatives.

Whitebread, D. and Coltman, P. (2015) *Teaching and learning in the early years* (4th edn.). London: Routledge.

Wijlaars, L. P. M. M., Gilbert, R. and Hardelid, P. (October 2016) Chronic conditions in children and young people: Learning from administrative data. *Archives of Disease in Childhood*, 101(10). Available at: https://adc.bmj.com/content/archdischild/101/10/881.full.pdf [Accessed: 22 December 2022].

Wilson, T. (2016) *Working with parents, carers and families in the early years: The essential guide.* London: Routledge.

Winton, P., Snyder, P., & Goffin, S. (2016). Beyond the status-quo: Rethinking professional development for early childhood teachers. In: L. Couse & S. Recchia (eds.), *Handbook of early childhood teacher education.* New York: Routledge, 54–68.

Wisbey, M. (2021) *Exploring the introduction of the Montessori method in a Malawian cultural context through collaborative action research with children and teachers.* Educational Doctorate. Anglia Ruskin University.

World Health Organization (2022) *Health and wellbeing.* Available at: https://www.who.int/data/gho/data/major-themes/health-and-well-being [Accessed: 6 November 2022].

Yerkes, M. A. and Javornik, J. (2019). Creating capabilities: Childcare policies in comparative perspective. *Journal of European Social Policy*, 29(4), 529–544.

INDEX

www.ingramcontent.com/pod-product-compliance
Lightning Source LLC
Chambersburg PA
CBHW080519030426
42337CB00023B/4567